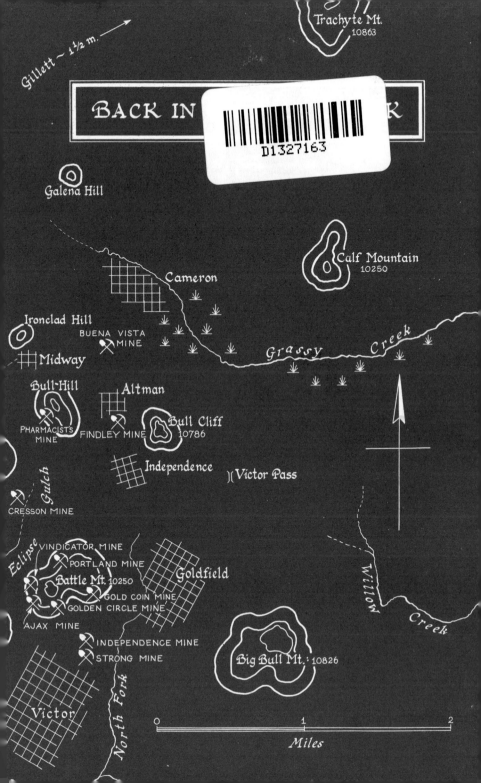

*by Mabel Barbee Lee*

BACK IN CRIPPLE CREEK

THE RAINBOW YEARS

AND SUDDENLY IT'S EVENING

CRIPPLE CREEK DAYS

# BACK IN CRIPPLE CREEK

# BACK IN CRIPPLE CREEK

## Mabel (Barbee) Lee

Doubleday & Company, Inc., Garden City, New York
1968

Chapters V and X originally appeared in somewhat different form, under the titles "The Phantom Bonanza of Battle Mountain" and "When the Kansas Tornado Struck Cripple Creek," in the anthology *Legends and Tales of the Old West.*

Chapter I originally appeared in somewhat different form in *Cripple Creek Days,* by Mabel Barbee Lee.

Excerpts from *Round by Round* by Jack Dempsey. Copyright 1940 by William Harrison Dempsey. Reprinted by permission of McGraw-Hill Book Company.

For My Friends
JOHN WOLCOTT STEWART
and
MARKA WEBB STEWART

Whose memories, like my own
are rooted in the plains and
high Rockies of Colorado

# INTRODUCTION
## By Lowell Thomas

Scattered all through the mountain country of our western states, the Rockies, the Sierra, and the many ranges between, there are hundreds of ghost towns. I doubt whether there is a valley anywhere in the Sangre de Cristo from Wyoming to New Mexico, or among the towering peaks of the San Juan, the Wasatch in Utah, the Sawtooth in Idaho, or the High Sierra of California, where there isn't evidence of the search for minerals, especially gold and silver.

A few of the most spectacular of these are now having a new boom. Skiers are bringing wealth back into these mountains, instead of going there to dig for it. By now everyone has heard of what has been happening at Aspen, where in mining days many fortunes were made in silver; the same recently at Vail, Colorado, in the Gore Mountain country. Thousands of others are skiing at Alta in Utah, with only a few realizing that in these mountains directly beneath their skis are hundreds of miles of abandoned tunnels and stopes. In the heart of the High Sierra, an almost forgotten area called Mineral King, once a gold camp, is about to be transformed into one of the world's larger ski resorts. All this of course will keep a few of the old mining towns from being utterly forgotten.

But one of the most exciting of them all, one with a

particularly lurid and dramatic past, will not soon be forgotten for other reasons. The Cripple Creek District near the top of the Front Range of the Colorado Rockies, may have no future as a ski area, because the weather man doesn't cooperate. The storms coming in from Canada, our Pacific Northwest, and from California, dump their snows on the mountains of Idaho, Utah, Wyoming, and the main range of the Rockies, while the Colorado Front Range gets what is left over. I can remember how at our home, up at ten thousand feet, our heaviest snows usually came in April, often in May, sometimes even in June.

However, today the Cripple Creek District is enjoying its own special boom. Texans and prosperous ranchers and farmers from Eastern Colorado, Nebraska, and Kansas, have bought up most of the buildings not torn down in the Twenties and Thirties when it became too expensive to mine and extract the gold from that "hard rock."

Then there's another reason why what we used to call "The World's Greatest Gold Camp" is not likely to be forgotten for at least a century or two. This is because of a gifted writer by the name of Mabel Barbee Lee, who now gives us her third book of stories about the days when she was a school girl and later a teacher in a gold mining camp where the population was made up of gamblers, girls of the red-light district, high-graders, prize fighters, overnight millionaires, and all the adventurers who in those days were attracted by the lure of gold.

As I read Mabel Barbee Lee's stories I get a rather special shock when she tells about Pearl De Vere, of the plush Old Homestead on Myers Avenue, who imported nearly everything, ball gowns as well as elaborate furnishings, from Paris, and the casual way she describes how she recently visited Two-Bit Lil down in Florence and got the story of how Lil became a girl "on the row." I also get a real kick out of hearing her tell about "French Blanche," "Token Tessie" Dunn, a gal named "Leo the Lion," the profanity of Peg Leg McGinty, and how my old friend Sam Vidler's wife shot Sam's friend Nellie.

Why do these stories shake me up a bit? Because, when I first knew Mabel Barbee Lee she was an ultra-feminine (she still is) beautiful young redhead, the youngest of my high school teachers, who wouldn't even look at the prostitutes we had to pass daily on our way to school. Little did I dream that lovely Mabel, in later life, would be reminding me of Crapper Jack's Dance Hall.

There was nothing at all about Mabel Barbee before she married a young mining engineer to suggest she might one day be writing stories about the wife of Sam Rankin, who owned the Diamond Saloon, where I sold newspapers, and sometimes put my earnings in the slot machines.

Later Sam was one of the principal owners of a daily newspaper I edited up there on top of the Rockies. Still later Mother Rankin, a widow, also retired to nearby Florence, Colorado, where above her hardware store she kept eleven or twelve bedrooms spotless and ready for the visits of "her boys"—who never came, except in the Forties when one became a popular Governor of Colorado. For some reason Ralph Carr and I down through the years had remained Mother Rankin's favorites, and on one occasion the Governor and I did make a pilgrimage to see her. She had at least a dozen pictures of the two of us on her walls, and Ralph and I were just about overcome by the tragedy and nostalgia of it all.

If someone had told us how Mabel Barbee Lee more than half a century later would be writing a book telling of her experiences with Jack Dempsey, and that she would be turning out a book whose pages would include references to "Big Jim" Jeffries, "Gentleman Jim" Corbett, "Ruby Bob"

Fitzsimmons, "Fireman Jim" Flynn, Tom "Sailor Boy" Sharkey, Jack Johnson, Stanley Ketchell, and other giants of that era, we would have fallen out of our seats laughing.

A few of Mabel Barbee Lee's stories concern friends of mine who remained in Colorado in the years long after I had taken off for Chicago, the East, and World War One. In one she gives us a graphic account of young Eddie Eagan (later amateur heavyweight champion of the world) startling the Cripple Creek miners in his fight with local white hope, Lum Myberg, who had been one of my schoolmates.

Nearly all these stories are about people I knew. But, she gives a full account of one both exciting and hilarious incident I missed. I guess it happened the year my mother took us East to visit relatives in Darke County, Ohio. That was when Carry Nation "the Kansas Tornado" swept into the gold camp with the threat, as Mabel Barbee tells it, "to smash every joint from Poverty Gulch to Squaw Mountain." This story she got from another of my old friends, Ben Hill, whose son instead of following his father as a mining engineer went to sea and became a U. S. Admiral. It all had to do with Johnny Nolon's ritzy saloon and gambling establishment, where above the bar there hung a rather startling nude "Venus Emerging from the Sea." Johnny made the mistake of inviting Carry Nation to drop in and entertain his customers with her temperance speech. What happens to Venus makes an exciting episode.

"The California Gold Rush had its Bret Harte, and the Klondike its Jack London and Robert Service. Rex Beach in *The Spoilers* tells us about the early days in Nome. Luckily Cripple Creek has its Mabel Barbee Lee."

# CONTENTS

# ACKNOWLEDGMENTS

My first book, *Cripple Creek Days* (Doubleday: 1958), consisted of my childhood recollections of the gold rush, supplemented by others of my generation with whom I spent countless hours in wonderful reminiscences. No two of us recalled the colorful, exciting, and sometimes tragical events of those years in quite the same detail. But we were agreed on the distinctive flavor of the famous old mining camp and the character of the men and women who flocked there, hoping to strike it rich.

The present book is a sequel, partly to my own story but mostly to the remembrances of others who lived on in the District long after I had married and gone away. It is written through the mellowed perspective of the young girl grown to mature womanhood. The interviews with old-timers and the notes taken from newspapers stored at the Carlton Mill were secured when I was making researches and gathering material for *Cripple Creek Days*. I have not forgotten all the friends, old and new, who shared their tales with me. Many of them have since died and gone to rest in Pisgah Graveyard. The countless letters from their families have reassured me and led me to this further selection of memoirs.

The sincere interest and help of Lowell Thomas is evident throughout my Cripple Creek books. No neophyte writer ever had a more faithful or inspiring friend. Words could not possibly express my appreciation. I am grateful to the old-timers still active in the District, who have taken the trouble to bring me up-to-date about the promising developments of the camp as an attractive summer resort; my thanks go especially to Postmaster and Mrs. Leslie Wilkinson, Mr. Francis W. Gunn, and Dr. A. C. Denman. I found the Diamond Jubilee edition of the *Cripple Creek Gold Rush* particularly informative and appealing. My salute to editor Roy G. Robinson, Jr.

It was a delight to hear again from Mrs. Norma Burbridge Hill, widow of Ben Hill, and to hear that she is living with the Troy Wades, her daughter and son-in-law, in Grand Junction, Colorado. It was a pleasure to get in touch with Mr. Bundy Colwell of Los Angeles, son of the late Mrs. Pearl O'Brien Colwell Olsen, one of the most beautiful young schoolteachers in early Cripple Creek. Her family was prominent in the mining life of the District and Mr. Colwell was kind enough to let me read excerpts from the diaries of his uncles; and also an article, published in the 1960 Brand Book of the Denver Westerners, by Raymond G. Colwell, the youngest of the brothers.

The second generation of the District's old-timers is also represented by Wallace Irwin, Jr., and his brother Donald, sons of the late Wallace Irwin, distinguished poet and novelist, and the late Mrs. Irwin. They generously permitted me to quote from a charming letter their father had written me in the mid-Fifties, telling, with typical Irwin humor, of his experiences as an eighteen-year-old assayer's helper at the Brodie Reduction Mill in Mound City, a budding "suburb" of Cripple Creek that died, like others, on the stem.

Thanks to Mrs. Carma D. Leigh, California State Librarian, Sacramento, the Denver Public Library, and the Santa Barbara Public Library for their ever-present aid in

[16]

times of trouble. I want also to express appreciation for Marshall Sprague's fine book about Cripple Creek, called *Money Mountain* (Little, Brown: 1953). It has been of endless value in checking slippery dates and sometimes the illusive spelling of names and places. I am grateful to Mr. Davis Dresser (Bret Haliday; "Michael Shane") in giving me wise counsel at a time of need.

The following books enabled me to find my way through the intricacies of prize fighting in Cripple Creek: *In the Ring and Out* by Jack Johnson (National Sports Publishing Co., Chicago: 1927). This fascinating autobiography was kindly loaned to me by Mr. and Mrs. Fred Mazzulla of Denver from their valuable collection of Western Americana. With permission of the authors or publishers, I have used excerpts from *Round by Round* by Jack Dempsey (McGraw-Hill Book Company: 1940); as well as excerpts from *Fighting for Fun* by the late Edward F. P. "Eddie" Eagan (Macmillan: 1943). Also, I am indebted to Alfred A. Knopf, Inc., for permission to use quotes from *Carry Nation* by Herbert Asbury (1929).

I cannot close *Back in Cripple Creek* without expressing heartfelt appreciation to Miss Marjorie T. Brown, who has been my third arm in countless ways, patiently and loyally devoting her spare hours from another full-time position, to type and help in the preparation of this manuscript and of my previous one, called *The Rainbow Years*. Thanks again, Margie!

*Mabel Barbee Lee*

*When Time who steals our years away*
*Shall steal our pleasures too*
*The mem'ry of the past will stay*
*And half our joys renew*

THOMAS MOORE, 1779–1852

# I

# Going Back Home

It had been more than thirty years since Howe, my husband, had died and almost five decades had passed since my graduation from Colorado College, in Colorado Springs. I was getting on, as my mother used to say, and my responsibilities had eased. More and more lately, my thoughts had been reverting to Cripple Creek, the famous mining camp in Colorado where I grew up. Stories had reached me from time to time about its disintegration. Soon it would be a ghost town, they said, a skeleton rattling its bones. The reports were that only a few old-timers were left in the District; newcomers from Texas and Oklahoma were buying up the best of the old houses for a few dollars to use for a month or two in the summer. It was difficult for me to imagine the throbbing, lustful camp of my childhood grown decrepit and I became obsessed with the idea of going back again before it crumbled in ruins.

When Howe died, I had myself and a young child to support, and after a few years trying to get my bearings, I returned to the field of education as Dean of Women at my Alma Mater. Then followed administrative positions at Radcliffe, Harvard Summer School, Bennington, Whitman, and finally the University of California in Berkeley. Before I realized it, 1951 had brought me to another milepost. The time had come to say good-by to the college campus and the signs at the crossroads were indistinct. I was conscious only of a longing to go home, back to the house on Golden Avenue in Cripple Creek. Beyond that was the dream of reliving the gold-rush years of my childhood and writing a book of memories about them. There was talk of developing the camp into a famous tourist attraction, on the order of Central City and Aspen, as a center of the arts with a museum, a dance group, and theater.

I would have to hurry, I thought, if I hoped to find Cripple Creek as I had once known it. But it was a long way from California to Colorado and my funds were short. I was on the verge of giving up the idea as being a risky, impractical venture when, out of the blue, a check came from Lowell Thomas, who had once been my pupil in the Victor High School and with whom I had always kept in touch, urging me to spend the summer renewing my youth in Cripple Creek. It was the push of confidence that I needed and I arranged to go at once.

The bus was crowded when it left Colorado Springs but gradually emptied as we stopped at the summer resorts up Ute Pass. I was the only passenger when we pulled out of Woodland Park, and I moved nearer to the driver, a fellow they called Nate, in order to dispel a strange sense of loneliness that had overcome me. The road climbed west from there, edging the foothills of Pike's Peak. Although it was the last of June, patches of snow still clung to the gulches.

Nearby, lupine, mustard, and candytuft tossed on the sunny hillsides and meadowlarks sang from the telephone wires.

"How far is it from here?" I asked Nate, "will it be much longer?" The last time I had come was on the Midland Terminal train.

"'Bout half or three-quarters of an hour," he replied, without looking around. "You a stranger in these parts?"

"Not exactly. I lived in Cripple Creek as a child and later taught school in Victor. I've been back only once or twice in the past fifty years. Are any pioneers left?"

"A few hundred." He seemed unimpressed. "Lotsa old-timers coming back these days. Guess they find good many changes. Sure ain't what it used to be."

I asked him if he would drive past the National Hotel. "I went to the big opening in 1896. It was a memorable event. Is it still there?"

He gave me an amused glance. "You sure are a new-comer. It was tore down in 1919. Only hotel today is the Imperial up on Third Street, opposite the old telephone building. Kinda hard gettin' a room there 'less you've got a reservation."

"What's going on?" I asked, a little apprehensive.

"The mellerdrama show in the basement, a real rootin', tootin' tearjerker. Tenderfeet flock up here by the hundreds, in Cadillacs an' Lincolns, to take it in an' do the other sights like goin' down the Molly Kathleen Mine. Gives 'em a big kick." He was silent a moment. "Come to think of it, though, today bein' Thursday they ain't usually so many. Maybe there'll be room for you. Hotel manager's a real nice accommodatin' fella, name's Mackin."

The Imperial had been a second-rate place in my youth, not in a class with the National Hotel in the center of camp just west of the Midland Depot. It acquired superior status only a decade ago when the Wayne Mackins, an enterprising

[23]

young couple, arrived in camp, with the idea of starting a summer theater. They bought the one and only hotel, refurbished it in period style, and made it the base of their operations.

I glanced around the lobby while Nate brought in my luggage. It had been fixed up more or less like an early-day hostelry, with large red leather chairs flanked by tall sand-filled cuspidors, as receptacles for cigar stubs and cigarette butts. Sports magazines and newspapers, including the weekly *Cripple Creek Gold Rush,* lay scattered on a console table standing against a wall. Through a door toward the back could be seen a large dining room with plaid gingham-covered tables and, as I turned away, the fragrance of freshly baked bread tickled my nostrils. The desk clerk, whom I presumed to be Mr. Mackin, was a tall, good-looking young man in his thirties, with balding hair and brown eyes. He held out his hand and smiled as I finished signing the register.

"I am Wayne Mackin," he said informally. "My wife, Dorothy, and I have heard about you through Mrs. A. W. Oliver, our Director of County Welfare up at the Court House."

"Oh, yes, I remember her well," I said cheerfully. "Her two pretty daughters were once my pupils in the Victor High School. One of them was a sweetheart of Lowell Thomas, a classmate."

"Mrs. Oliver told me," he went on, "that Lowell had written to her you might be showing up in camp one of these days to get material for a book you were going to write about the District. That's fine. If we can be of any help, let us know."

"My main concern just now," I said, "is to find a place where I can live for a few weeks—maybe a couple of months. Do you think you could put me up here at the Imperial?"

His smile quickly vanished as he scanned the list of reservations. "You couldn't have arrived at a worse time," he said. "All of our weekends are booked up to the rafters right through July. It would mean that you would have to be moving in and out all the time, if you lived here."

My spirits sank. "Could you suggest another hotel or an apartment or possibly a room in a private home?"

He nodded regretfully. "To tell the truth, I don't know of another place in camp. I could put you up for tonight and that's about it. I'd suggest that you get in touch with Mrs. Oliver right away. She knows everyone in the District, on or off relief." I managed a faint smile at his humor. "Meanwhile, I'll phone around and between the two of us, something ought to be found."

I was tempted for a moment to leave word for Nate that I would return to Colorado Springs on the morning bus. Perhaps I could accomplish my purpose just as well, I thought, by commuting up here once or twice a week. Still, it wouldn't be the same as living steadily in camp, meeting the people and coming to know some of them. I decided that it would be better to talk the problem over with Mrs. Oliver before running away from what seemed to be a hopeless situation. I stood in front of the hotel trying to get my bearings before heading down the hill to Bennett Avenue. Only the old telephone building across the way looked familiar. All of a sudden my heart began to pound. Over the glass, in the upper part of the door, was the name in large black letters, Hoot Mon Apartments. I hurried over to see if I could arouse anyone.

After quite a wait, a buxom elderly woman with crimped gray hair, wearing a white starched apron and speaking with a Scotch accent, came to the door. "I am looking for an apartment," I said, "where I might live for several weeks. I hope you may have something available. I am an old-timer—perhaps you are a pioneer yourself. Somehow your face looks a bit familiar to me. Would you mind telling me your name?"

"Dewar," she said hesitantly, as if afraid of strangers. "Agnes Dewar. I've lived here in this building with my brother Jack for forty years, ever since the telephone people sold it. What did you say your name was?"

"Barbee," I said. "I was a young girl here and my name was Mabel Barbee." Agnes looked puzzled for a moment and said she didn't remember me.

"Maybe Jack will know you. He got around a lot more than I did."

"Oh, I recall Jack," I said warmly. "He used to get dressed up in his kilt and play the bagpipes in all the big Labor Day and Fourth of July parades. He was a handsome young fellow with dimples and blue eyes. Is he home today?"

"No, he ain't home. He's got a little souvenir stand down on Bennett Avenue where the tourists can buy specimens from all the big mines. Maybe you'd want to buy some to take home."

"I'll certainly do that, but first I'd be glad to know if there are any rooms available for me here at the Hoot Mon." She shook her head ominously. I was beginning to feel that this might be a common gesture so far as my finding a place to live was concerned.

"We have only two apartments," she said, "the one up-stairs—it's been rented to a man for a long time, and the one downstairs toward the back—it's where Jack and I live. We don't have anything for rent," and with that, she slowly started to close the door. I put my hand on her arm and said: "Wait a minute! If your tenant should leave before the end of summer, won't you please give me the refusal of his apartment? I'll pay you very well . . ."

[26]

Her eyes began to twinkle a bit and she smiled for the first time. "I'll have to ask Jack about it," she said. "He may remember you, but he's seventy-five now and he don't recollect people too well any more. I'll let you know if there's ever a vacancy."

I started down the street. Except for the south or shady side where half-demolished structures left gaping cavities, everything looked dimly familiar. Many of the buildings, although appearing tired and beaten, still flaunted their fading names: Burnside, Welty, Shockey, Phenix (the spelling had been shortened for lack of space), and Pullen. The Midland Depot across the east end dominated the downtown area. It stood aloof and dignified as always despite its sagging steps and boarded-up windows. It was planned, someone told me, to make it into a museum where mementos of Cripple Creek's glorious past would be displayed.

I cut across lots to Myers Avenue. It had been dubbed "Julian Street" after the author by that name wrote a scurrilous article for *Collier's* magazine, picturing Cripple Creek as a vast tenderloin presided over by one "Leo the Lion," a denizen of the red-light district. Now it was nobody's street. Not a saloon, crib, or dance hall remained in the two blocks which once pulsated with music and gusty laughter. Only the two-storied pink brick lair of sin, "The Old Homestead," remained there, naked and alone, a monument to Cripple Creek's most profligate and debauched era. It was rumored that somebody had bought it recently, intending to put in extra baths and rent rooms named after former madames: Pearl, Hazel, Grace, Georgia-Belle, as added spice for the tourist trade.

I returned to Bennett Avenue, thinking I might find some old men on the street who would remember my father. Expensive cars were parked bumper to bumper along the sidewalk. Sauntering visitors stopped occasionally to gaze at the souvenirs in the small-shop windows. Several taverns enlivened the air with popular jukebox records. Through the swinging doors, customers could be glimpsed dressed in wide sombreros, high boots, and Levi's and sipping drinks, affecting the manners of the wild gold-rush years.

All of a sudden, I caught sight of an aged fellow leaning against the front of a vacant store and hurried over to speak to him, confident that the mention of John Barbee would bring a smile of recollection to the wrinkled unshaven face. "Have you been in Cripple Creek many years?" I asked brightly.

"Since spring of ninety-six," he replied, chewing his gums. "Came in as a kid after the big fires."

"Oh," I said, feeling let down, "you were too young then to know my father, John Barbee."

"Nope, never heard of 'im."

I went on to another feeble codger dozing in a sunny doorway. "I beg your pardon," I began politely, "I'm trying to find someone who might have known my father, John Barbee, in the early days. Sometimes he was called 'Honest John.'"

He squinted at me with watery eyes. "You his girl?"

My spirits rose. "Yes. I'm Mabs. I used to go prospecting with him summers over on Beacon Hill."

"I'm gettin' so my hearin's not much good. Wat'd you say his name was—Beacon?"

"Barbee—John Barbee," I shouted.

"Nope. Ain't seen 'im around lately; in fact never heard of a fella named Tom Barley." I made one or two further attempts and then gave up, convinced that my father had vanished from Cripple Creek's memory as completely as if he had never existed.

I started up to the County Court House on the corner of First Street where Mrs. Oliver had her office. She greeted me cordially, saying that Lowell had told her to look out for me. She was a remarkable person at age seventy-nine, rather stout, pleasant-faced, and full of information. I told her about my housing problem and said that I had even considered returning to Colorado Springs. But she immediately put in a word against it. "Don't leave now," she objected, "we're bound to find something before tomorrow night." She said that she would get on the phone right away and ask all her friends if they knew of anyone who had a room for rent. "There're always such crowds in camp over the weekend that I'm sure you wouldn't have any luck in Cripple Creek. But if we can't find anything here, maybe there'll be a better chance over in Victor."

We chatted a few moments about some of the old-timers who were still around who might like to recall early times. "By the way," I asked, "do you know whatever became of Oscar Burnside? He might have some very interesting tales to tell." Oscar Burnside owned the saloon where my father spent most of his money in liquor and gambling and I grew up with my mother's bitter hatred of all saloonkeepers. Naturally enough, he was the first one who came to mind when I returned to the camp.

"Old Man Burnside, poor fellow!" she said reminiscently. "He suffered plenty for his crimes against others. He died a number of years ago—had been sick and crippled with rheumatism for a long, long time. A.W. (Mr. Oliver was always called by his first initials) used to take him tobacco and relief groceries every week over to his little shack on the placer. Mrs. Burnside flew high for a while during the prosperous days, put on a lot of dog, and Blanche, their daughter, didn't have too good a name. Used up all the money Oscar had and more, I guess. Then the girl and her mother both died, leaving the old man penniless and alone. He passed away at the County Poor Farm and was buried at Pisgah Graveyard. The camp collected enough money to keep him out of the Potter's Field."

It was still early and I decided to walk up the steep street to Golden Avenue. I'd know our old house at once, I thought, for unlike the neighbors' homes which had been built by real carpenters after the fires, ours was literally thrown together by my father's unskilled hands and it leaned slightly westward. But I looked in vain for the block on Golden Avenue where I had played as a child. It was rubble. The only relic of those years was the Baltzell place, which the neighbors had helped to build. All the others had been torn down and the lumber sold to people in Florence and Cañon City.

I gazed out over the beautiful view beyond: Mount Pisgah, the distant Sangre de Cristo, the tips of the Collegiate Peaks to the northwest, the bald pate of Pike's Peak, and all of the surrounding gold-laden mountains that had poured their treasure into greedy pockets: Bull Hill, Raven, Beacon where my father had discovered the vein of the rich El Paso mine, only to be forced to sell it because of his health. Back toward the north lay Mineral Hill with its false hopes and dreams forever blasted. Gold had never yet been discovered on that mysterious mountain, but men continued prospecting it, certain that someday they would discover a bonanza.

Pisgah Graveyard spread out fantastically as the town shrank closer into the basin. My mother and father were buried there in the early 1900s. I decided to walk the mile or so to the gates. Toward the center of what looked like a vast wasteland of sunken graves, I saw a patch of green surrounded by an iron fence. It was the well-kept Masonic plot where my parents were buried and I sat down on a low tombstone nearby to rest.

How still it was! Not a breeze was stirring nor a creature. Not even a chipmunk. As far as one could see there were slanting headboards or granite slabs. Only sagebrush and scrubby spruce trees here and there relieved the bleakness and yet I felt a peaceful kind of beauty about the place that made it seem a haven for the strange breed of men and women who had once tramped the hills in search of treasure and fought and laughed and wept together. Now they were at rest on this wind-blown slope, the good and the bad, the evil and the saintly. Oscar Burnside, Pearl De Vere, and all the others whom my mother scorned and hated because she thought they were wicked people—now all had become reconciled in death.

Suddenly from out of nowhere a blue jay lit on a post of the iron fence and began to scold, as if to remind me that the sun was setting behind Mount Pisgah and that I had better be going back to the hotel before the chill of the late afternoon set in. I picked my way among the rocks and sunken mounds and looked back for a moment in farewell to my parents' graves. Beacon Hill rose to the south and the El Paso Mine lay in full view. The great producer, too, was dead, together with the prospector who discovered it.

I quickened my steps down the dusty road to camp, so lost in thought that it startled me to hear someone speaking. It was a gray-bearded man wearing a corduroy coat that looked as if he had come in with the gold rush. I forgot to ask if he had known my father; somehow it didn't matter any more.

"Nice day for a walk," he was saying. "Don't see strangers footin' it 'round here often any more."

"Are you prospecting in this area?" I asked, noticing the small canvas ore sack in his coat pocket.

"Yep, on Mineral Hill," he said, pointing in that direction. "Got a good claim up there—"

"But I understand most of the big strikes were at the opposite end of camp, on Battle Mountain and Beacon Hill,"

I said. "What makes you think you'll find gold on Mineral Hill?"

"Say, you talk just like any other tenderfoot!" he chuckled. "Well, let me tell you somethin'. See that flat bit a land yonder? In the early days it was a placer—Freeman's placer. I seen nuggets panned outa there big as chestnuts. Couldn't come from nowheres, I figgered, 'cept Mineral Hill—washed down hundreds a years ago. I gotta claim that'll prove it. Won't be long 'til I open up the biggest lode ever found in the District. Take it from me, this ol' minin' camp's a long ways yet from cashin' in its chips. Come back again pretty soon," he added, turning to go, "when things are boomin'. Could be pretty soon now!"

The shine of hope and faith in the old fellow's eyes followed me long after he had disappeared from sight. And it came to me, as it had once long ago, when I went prospecting with my father, that it wasn't the gold he wanted. It would likely slip through his fingers in no time or be given away for the asking. It was the enticing hunt that led him on, the elusive chase, the everlasting love of the game.

I hardly realized that I had reached the hotel, so lost in thought was I about the old fellow who was so sure he would strike a bonanza on Mineral Hill.

Mr. Mackin was waiting with a message from Mrs. Oliver, saying that she had found a place for me in Victor, in the McMillin Building over the mortuary. If I wanted it, she said, I should let her know so that A.W. could pick me up the next afternoon when he came to take her home from the office. I was so happily relieved at the news that I decided to indulge in one of François' extravagant dinners and afterward go down to The Gold Bar Room Theatre in the basement to see the play. It was a heart-rending melodrama about a beautiful innocent girl led astray by an evil gambler. The audience hissed the villain and pounded their beer mugs on the tables at his entrances and exits. They cheered the brave hero and called out words of hope and encouragement to the lovely heroine as the villain tightened her lisle stocking around her throat.

I've never been very fond of beer but I thought I would order a mug to see if it wouldn't put me in the spirit of gaiety and abandonment. Everything seemed phony and unreal, the homemade props, the amateur actors, the slightly tipsy audience, and the tinny piano playing "Hearts and Flowers" as the heroine fainted and was rescued by the hero.

Cripple Creek, the new tourist resort, was about to become an old ghost town and I, who since childhood had feared everything connected with death, crepes on doors, corpses, and graveyards, was about to settle down in a room in Victor, over a mortuary, to gather up my memories of the gold-rush years.

# II

# The Camp of Ghosts

The Olivers called for me early the next afternoon so that there would be plenty of time, they said, to drive the long way, up over Bull Hill and Bull Cliff to Victor. "The road is none too good and it's pretty steep in places," A.W. warned. "You may recognize it as the old, electrified inter-urban route, called the High Line."

I had never met A.W. before, and although he boasted of being eighty-three, his manner was alert and pleasing and there were marks of distinction in his handsome face. "We'll take it slowly," he went on, "and if the engine overheats, we can stop awhile and drink in the spectacular views—"

"That reminds me, A.W.," Mrs. Oliver said anxiously, "did you remember to fill the Thermos bottle with mint juleps?"

"By George—I clean forgot 'em!" he said, giving me a mischievous wink and then added, "Viola, my beloved wife, would rather trade scenery any day for one of my mint juleps!"

We started up Tenderfoot Hill from where I had entered

Cripple Creek by bus the day before. But instead of following the macadamized highway to Ute Pass, we branched off and turned south, climbing the east slopes of Globe and Ironclad Hills, curving around Bull Cliff with its ruins of Midway, one of the earliest camps in the District, and finally reaching the summit of Bull Hill where we stopped to sample A.W.'s mint juleps and enjoy the panorama. Off to a side, half-hidden in scraggly sagebrush, was a faded sign which read:

*Altman, Colorado*
*1891–1905*
*Highest incorporated town*
*in the United States*
*Altitude 10,650 ft.*
*Destroyed by fire 5-23-'05*

"It must have been a mighty lively place in the Nineties," I said. "I was pretty young then and don't remember much about it."

"I landed here a little later," A.W. said, "but I've been told that at one time two thousand miners and their families lived in this area. It was local headquarters for the Western Federation of Miners. They kept mine owners in continual hot water, trying to fight demands for a minimum wage of three dollars for an eight-hour shift. Things came to a showdown in the strike of 1894 when Bull Hill was turned into a fortress with great guns nosing down the mountain toward Cripple Creek, ready to blow the town to smithereens unless the miners' rights were granted. The mine owners were practically without guns or ammunition or even political support and they soon gave in. After that the minimum wage and hour law became a fixture in the District's labor disputes." A.W. adjusted the fresh pansy in his buttonhole and lit a cigar. "It was found afterward," he went on, "that

[35]

the 'heavy artillery' of the Bull Hill fortress, which had scared the daylights out of everybody in camp, had been made of tree trunks, stovepipes, and paint."

We roared with laughter at the miners' stratagem. "Just think," Viola said, wiping her eyes, "all that's left of Altman is that old sign, a couple of my feeble asthmatics on relief, and a view that A.W. claims can't be beat anywhere in the Rockies."

Snow glistened in the thin air on the Sangre de Cristo far away to the Southwest. The wind-swept dome of Pike's Peak appeared only a stone's throw across the grassy meadows of Beaver Park which fringed the foothills. We drove down the lower slopes past tottering mine sheds and prospect holes to Independence, where Harry Orchard, the arch-killer, once lived. He had helped to set off the depot explosion, during the strike of 1903–4, that brought death to thirteen nonunion workers waiting on the platform after the night shift for the Midland Terminal train to take them home.

"You can still see the wreckage," A.W. said, pointing. "Those were hard days and nobody won the fight. The Western Federation of Miners lost the strike and the District lost its life. It began to go downhill from 1903 on—nothing was ever the same again."

The gouged-out shell of Battle Mountain rose just ahead marking our approach to Victor. It was crisscrossed by countless roads and well-worn trails circling the sprawling waste heaps of Stratton's Independence; the Portland a few hundred feet away; the Ajax; Strong; Granite, and many other famous producers.

Because of this gold-rich mountain, Victor, which lay at its base, was called "The City of Mines." I had often looked out on the scene from my classroom window, long ago, in the High School. It all suddenly returned in memory. Miners hurrying down the trails, flashing their lunch buckets in the waning sun. Waste spilling from ore cars and rattling dryly over the dumps. Heavy, brown smoke billowing from the huge stacks and flattening in fantastic shapes against the sky. Somewhere from behind Squaw Mountain a phantom train whistle. "You know," I said to A.W., "we haven't passed another car all the way over from Cripple Creek!"

"Only old-timers know about the Bull Hill cutoff," Viola put in. "Tourists take the paved road that used to be the electrified interurban Low Line as far as the Carlton Mill. After they've paid a dollar to go through and see the synthetic gold bricks, they speed back to the Creek without ever coming on to Victor."

We had driven down a steep hill past Mrs. Foster's boardinghouse where I had first met Howe, whom I later married. It had become a shambles, almost crushed apart by the merciless, restless dump of the Granite Mine. Farther along the slope was the old-fashioned, wine-red Midland Terminal Depot with its familiar wide, overhanging eaves and bumpy platform. Now there were no rails, no traffic to mark its importance to the town. "There has been talk recently that Lowell Thomas is thinking of buying it for a summer home, just so that he could look out the window every morning and see the fabulous Sangre de Cristo shimmering in the sun, a hundred miles away in New Mexico," A.W. commented.

"Victor was his boyhood home," I said. "He had many happy memories of it and returns whenever he gets a chance. He'll be glad, I'm sure, when he hears that Viola found an apartment for me in the McMillin Block."

But misgivings gripped me when A.W. pulled up in front of a two-story brick building on North Second Street and said, as he tightened the brake, "Well, girls, here we are. I hope

[37]

you're not as tuckered out as the old man! That High Line is a hard road to drive."

"You just sit in the auto and rest a bit," Viola said. "Mabel and I can manage the suitcases all right."

Apparently it was the only occupied structure around and stood like a forbidding guard against newcomers. A steep central stairway separated the two large rooms facing the sidewalk on the ground floor. On the padlocked door of one was a "For Rent" sign that looked as if it had hung there since the gold rush. The other housed the undertaking parlor. The sight of the dark green funereal blinds covering the windows sent a shudder through me. The sickening thought came to me that I was about to make my home in an apartment over a mortuary.

"Are there any cadavers in there now?" I asked Viola.

"Only those two young fellows that were killed yesterday in an auto accident over on Four Mile Hill." She gave me a searching glance. "I hope you're not afraid of corpses!"

"Of course not," I lied. "I was just wondering—"

"Don't worry," she said, smiling reassuringly. "At least you will have nice quiet neighbors; your rest tonight won't be disturbed. Then, as if trying to cheer me up a bit, she added, "Grace Eads—she's Norris' widow—has fixed up a lovely apartment just across the hall from yours. She's about A.W.'s age and will be lots of company for you when she returns from her visit in the Springs." We put down the luggage and I urged her to hurry back to A.W. waiting in the car. "Remember now," she called out, "if you need any help, just run down to Mame's Café on the corner of Victor Avenue and phone us up."

I was glad to be alone, at last, and free to look around at my quarters. It didn't take long. They consisted of one fairly large room in front, with a tiny kitchenette to one side that looked as though it had once been a clothes closet.

A thin, lumpy mattress lay on the single springs of an old-fashioned iron bedstead. Several blankets and sheets were piled on a center table nearby. A lone electric light was suspended from the ceiling and someone had tied it with a string to the small mirror on the dresser.

The shattering thought occurred to me, all at once, that the McMillin Building might go up in flames any time. I was a girl of twelve when two devastating fires, within three days of each other, almost wiped out Cripple Creek, and the experience forever left its mark on me. If there was anything that I dreaded more than a mortuary with its carbolic smell of death, it was the fear of being burned alive in some rattletrap hotel or apartment house. I decided at once to look for the fire escape. A door near the rear turned out to be a public bathroom and toilet. I turned the knob of another door at the end of a long corridor. A hand-printed sign at one side read: "Emergency Exit." But instead of an iron stairway leading down, there was only the empty space of a wide stretch of land, fifty feet below, where the Victor Grand Opera House once stood. The charred foundations gave mute evidence that it had gone the way of the District's other opera houses.

On a high hill a couple of blocks east loomed the stately brick High School where once I had been a teacher. The memory of it brought a sardonic smile. Before climbing the rocky road to classes, faculty members and pupils alike had to pass a row of cribs, called "the line," which cowered in the shadow of the Opera House. Victor's tenderloin was every bit as disreputable as that on Myers Avenue, but it was not so widely known for parlor houses like the Old Homestead. School children ignored its existence unless some unusual commotion, such as hair-pulling females, attracted attention. Today there was no vestige of the red-light district. Nothing was left but the high-school building which towered like a perennial symbol of promise and hope. But nowhere, inside or out of the McMillin Block, had I found a fire escape!

I went back to my apartment, resolved to move to a safer place at the first opportunity. Meanwhile, I'd try to make the best of things. I unpacked some of my clothes and hung them on the wall racks. I made the bed and turned on the light. It was not yet five o'clock, but the sun had disappeared behind Squaw Mountain and dusk was settling over the town. I began to feel hungry and went to Mame's Café for supper. It was a surprisingly neat place, free of the usual odor of stale garbage. A man had just put a coin in a huge jukebox which was flashing colored lights and banging out an old, familiar rag, called "Bibbidi—Bobbidi—Boo."

Suddenly I realized that the man was Nate. He had sat down on a stool at the lunch counter and was attacking a heaped-up plate of food and washing it down with frequent draughts of beer. I greeted him as if he were my long-lost brother and pulled up the stool next to him. He grinned broadly as if surprised to see me and said he had wondered how I had made out at the Imperial. I told him my troubles and confessed that I had been on the verge of going back to Colorado Springs with him on the next trip, when Mrs. Oliver found an apartment for me in Victor, in the McMillin Block.

"Good God!" he exclaimed. "That's where she sends folks on relief! Mrs. Norris Eads has the only decent rooms in the whole building. I was thinkin' that you were lookin' for a swell joint, like the Imperial, or I'd a-told you about the Hackley Hotel, across the street from Mame's here. It's where I hole up nights. The bus leaves from the Hackley at eight every mornin'—makes it right convenient for me." He took a long, deep swig of beer. "It's cheap, too. You might get a room there that'd suit you better 'n that dump over the undertaking parlor. Still—the Hackley's a firetrap. I fully expect to find it burned to the ground one of these days when I come back from the Springs. I don't know as I'd recommend it to a lady."

"Oh, I'll be all right in the McMillin apartment," I said hastily, hoping to forestall another discussion of the Hackley. Somehow, that threat about it being a firetrap gave a kind of luster even to the mortuary. I thanked Nate for his interest but said I was more or less settled. "By the way," I added, anxious to change the subject, "do you happen to pass by the Carlton Mill when you go mornings to Cripple Creek and Colorado Springs? I don't know just where it is and I'll doubtless need transportation."

"Sure as shootin'. I always stop there to pick up the mail." He turned on the stool and stared at me questioningly. "For cripes' sake, don't tell me you're aimin' to look for a room there!"

I explained how I had arranged to read the old Cripple Creek and Victor newspapers which were stored for safe-keeping in the attic of the mill. "I'm going to write a book," I said, "about the gold rush, but fifty years is a long time to remember back. I need to get into the atmosphere of the early days, to read about all the excitement and recall the big events. I want to find out what kind of clothes we wore, and what food we ate. I shall be after local color, a lot of local color and there's no better hunting for it than in the old newspapers!"

Nate listened as if spellbound. "Well, what d'you know," he said at last, "a real live author knockin' around in the mill, readin' about the early days in the Crik. Baby, if you ever get stuck for juicy news that never made the papers, just call on yours truly. I got two or three ol'-timer frien's still livin' down in Florence. Might take ya there if you ever want to go." Two things had become plain to me: Nate had drunk too many beers and his conversation had grown too cozy for comfort. I hurried through my dish of liver and onions, paid Mame the check, and promised Nate to be at the Hackley corner at eight on Monday morning.

I had read about the dedication of the Carlton Mill several years before in the Denver *Post*. It had been built by Ethel, the widow of A. E. "Bert" Carlton, the multimillionaire mine owner and developer of the Cripple Creek District. It was speculated that great quantities of gold could be recovered with proper treatment from the dumps of former bonanzas. Victor and Cripple Creek were a little over six miles apart and the mill hugged Arequa Gulch just halfway between the two towns below the deserted camp of Elkton. Already its yellow tailings had fanned out almost a mile to the lower slopes of Guyot Hill and Squaw Mountain. And gold bricks were being shipped every week to mints in Denver or Salt Lake City or San Francisco. The Carlton dream of one day owning every great mine in the Cripple Creek District had long since been realized, with the exception of the Strong, above Victor, and now Ethel was wringing the last traces of gold from their mammoth dumps.

When I arrived the first morning, Mr. A. N. "Bob" Ragle, business manager of the mill, took me up to the attic to show me the magnitude of the task I was about to tackle. Great piles of dusty clothbound newspapers lay scattered over the cement floor. "Quite a few folks who claimed they were going to write books about Cripple Creek's gold rush have been here to take a look at the old newspapers," Bob said, snapping on the lone electric light and smiling skeptically. "They never stayed more than a few hours, or at most a day. I figure it would take a whole summer to do the job justice."

I wondered if he were trying to discourage me, and hastily said, "That is exactly what I expect to do. All I need is a chair and a table and a little bigger light globe." He seemed pleased, and promised he would clear out an office for me on the ground floor and that he would be glad to carry the files down each day, as I wanted them—two or three at a time. "There's a large window in front," he added, "and I'll see that nobody disturbs you."

"Your kindness," I said, "makes me apologetic for asking you still another question, but perhaps you could tell me of a millworker, who lives in Victor, with whom I could drive back to camp at the end of the day." When I told him that I had an apartment in the McMillin Block, he said that he was putting up at the Hackley Hotel temporarily and that I could ride with him until he and his wife moved into the Old Homestead over in Cripple Creek. "We've bought the place," he went on, "and plan to modernize it and furnish the rooms upstairs for renting. Maybe we can hit a tourist jackpot like the Mackins up at the Imperial."

"When will it be ready?" I asked, perking up my ears.

"Three or four weeks, we hope, but you can't tell. Labor and supplies are hard to come by these days, especially in the tourist season."

"Put me down for the first reservation," I said, half in amusement, "but keep it dark. My dear mother would rise from her grave in Pisgah if she ever got word that her daughter had finally landed in the Old Homestead!"

It was a disappointment to find that no files of the Cripple Creek *Morning Times* were available until after 1896. That was the year of the great fires, which destroyed most of the camp, including the newspaper plant and all its records. But as I gently turned the musty pages of later times, the sounds and sights, the lay of the land, the rancid smell of beer in the alleys, the Labor Day parades, the big funerals with the Elks Band heading the cortege—all came back to me vividly as if indelibly stamped on my memory. The early newspapers were not essential to a child not yet in her teens.

My first school was in a log cabin over in Old Town.

The floor was of dirt and the cold winter wind whistled through the door cracks and I was sick most of the time. It was 1893, the year my brother, Billie, was born in the tent over on Freeman's Placer. The second school was not much better. Buildings in camp must have been scarce, for it was in a sheet-iron structure next to Crapper Jack's Dance Hall and across from the row of cribs on Myers Avenue. It was a thrilling experience, at first, to amble past scantily dressed women, sitting in their wedge-shaped windows, smoking cigarettes. The boys would snicker and wink at each other knowingly and the girls would blush and turn away and quicken their steps. Before long, we came to know by sight such gaudy characters as Mexican Jennie, Leo the Lion, French Blanche, and Two-Bit Lil. Often they enlivened our recess periods with their noisy, profane brawls.

In pondering these fantastic days, it occurred to me that some of the former denizens of Myers Avenue might still be alive and even within reach of Cripple Creek. The more I thought about it, the more excited I became and one morning when I was Nate's only passenger, I asked him if he knew whether any of these old prostitutes were left in the District and even jogged his recollections by naming a few of them. "Leo the Lion is dead," he said, rather matter-of-factly. "Folks made it pretty tough for her, I heard, after she gave that fella, Julian Street, the lowdown on the Crik's tenderloin. It was all wrote up in some magazine. Myers Avenue don't exist no more—it's called Julian Street. That's funny," he laughed, "'cause it ain't even a street now—only a road. Nothin' there but the Ol' Homestead." He shifted into high, sat back in his seat and rolled a cigarette. "Come to think of it, Two-Bit Lil's down in Florence. What a gal she was—why, she could outcuss the toughest mule skinner!"

Florence was about thirty miles south of Victor. It was

[44]

where my mother and I changed from the train to the Concord stagecoach that took us up the Shelf Road in Phantom Canyon when we first came to Cripple Creek. Three years later, in 1895, the Denver & Rio Grande Railroad ran a narrow-gauge spur through Phantom Canyon, to win the initial race with the broad-gauge Colorado Midland Terminal pushing in from the north, for the District's fabulous shipping business. By the turn of the century, three steam railroads and two electric interurban lines served the District, winding among the hills, bridging the gulches, climbing ten thousand feet to Bull Cliff and Altman.

"How does one get to Florence today?" I asked. "Is the Shelf Road still open for traffic?" Already a plan was taking root in my mind.

"Hell, no! That suicide trail crumbled away a long time ago. Trucks that go down now and then have to follow the old D & R G roadbed, but a lotta that gets washed out ever' time it rains, an' nothin's sure about gettin' through." He looked at me quizzically for a moment and then smiled. "You aimin' to pay Two-Bit Lil a visit?"

I nodded absently, wondering how I could get transportation. "Do the trucks ever take a rider along?"

" 'Casionally. Some fella maybe, but no women folks. If you're game, why don't ya get Bob Ragle to fix it so's you can hook a ride down to the Valley, someday, in one of the mill trucks. It only takes about an hour an' a half goin' down, an' the Greyhound from Salt Lake 'll bring you back to the Springs in time to catch the afternoon bus for the Crik."

I laughed. "I might just do that. And if you miss me some morning soon, you'll know that I've kidnapped the driver of a mill truck and we're somewhere in Phantom Canyon bound for Florence and Two-Bit Lil!"

"So long!" he chuckled. "Be sure to give Lil my best!"

[45]

# III

# A Call on Two-Bit Lil

My desire to make the trip to Florence materialized sooner than expected. I mentioned it to Bob Ragle, as Nate had suggested, and he said that one of the Carlton trucks was going down to the Arkansas Valley the next morning to pick up a load of mill supplies. "Pete, the driver, would be glad to have your company, I'm sure, but you'd better wear old clothes," he warned. "It's a dusty, rough trip."

"That won't bother me," I replied rather testily. "I traveled the Shelf Road in a stagecoach before you were born. I'm no stranger to Phantom Canyon!"

We left from the Hackley corner at around six o'clock. Pete, a good-looking young fellow with long dark lashes that any girl would envy, was a native of Victor and had attended high school for two years when he quit to go to war. He had a wife and two children who lived in Cañon City, not far from Florence, and he made the trip down every week to see them. "I always stay overnight," he said, "and sometimes, if I'm lucky, a little longer."

I had been watching the road like a hawk, shifting gears and unconsciously putting on the brakes. Much of Pete's talk went unheeded until he suddenly said something about spending the night with his family.

"Aren't you going to return to the District this afternoon?" I asked anxiously. "I really hadn't counted on—"

"Guess Bob Ragle forgot to tell you—I never make the round trip in a day. Coming down the Canyon's not so bad, but man alive! with a load of nuts and bolts I have to play it in low most of the way back. It's pretty steep, you know—"

"I wonder if I could thumb a ride with somebody else."

"Mighty slim chance," he put in. "Your best bet would be to flag the Greyhound from Salt Lake that comes through Florence around noon. It will take you as far as the Springs. Nate's usually on hand there to pick up any transfers for the Creek. It's a nice trip," he added. "Only thing is, it takes about twice as long." He turned and looked at me curiously. "Florence is only a little town. Don't you know anybody there?"

I hesitated, not knowing quite what to say. "In a way, I do. It's someone I haven't seen for almost sixty years. I don't even know just how to find her. Certainly I couldn't spend the night. Her name is Lil Powers and she used to live in Cripple Creek—"

"Oh, you mean 'Two-Bit Lil'! Everybody in town knows where her place is. I'd better let you off at the corner by the hardware store—that's where you can hail the Greyhound—and then you walk straight down Main Street 'til you come to the railroad crossing. Her house is on the other side of the tracks—you can't miss it. It's painted like imitation brick. So long," he added, with a new sly note of familiarity, "I'll be seeing you!"

Florence was still a village, not much larger than it was

[47]

when my mother and I waited there for the Cripple Creek stage in 1892. I had no trouble finding Lil's place. It seemed to dominate the whole town. It was a large, sprawling building and looked more like a worn-out rooming house than a brothel. A sign on the front door read: CLOSED BY ORDER OF THE SHERIFF OF FREMONT COUNTY, followed by a statement of penalty for violation of the law. Evidently Lil was in trouble. However, I had come too far to be deterred by a sheriff's order. Besides, I felt that I looked respectable and I knew that my motives were pure. I knocked loudly several times and was aware of eyes peering from behind the lace curtains. At last I heard footsteps and saw the door open and an old woman with tight lips and a forbidding voice said: "Yes—what'd you want—didn't you see that notice? I'm not in business any more. Go away!"

I put on my most beguiling smile and told her that I was an old-timer from Cripple Creek, who attended school in the sheet-iron building across from where she lived on Myers Avenue. I went on to say that I was writing a book about the gold-rush years and wanted to talk with her of the early days. Immediately a wide relieved grin spread over her wrinkled face and she relaxed the clutch on her bizarre kimono and invited me in. She was a heavy-set woman with streaked gray hair, slicked back hastily, and her eyes were keen and twinkling.

"Well, I'll be damned," she began. "Feature seein' one of you pesky brats after all these years!" She pulled up a chair for me by the table. "I didn't mind the girls—I sorta felt sorry for 'em havin' to go to school in that hellhole. It was the nasty little boys, throwin' rocks at my window, yellin' dirty names—I wanted to wring their necks!" The smell of coffee drifted from the kitchen. "I ain't had my second cup yet," she said, bringing in the pot and setting it on the table. "Maybe you'd like one, too."

It was still early, only nine o'clock, but it seemed a long time since I'd had a quick cup of coffee at Mame's Café, before climbing onto Pete's truck, and I was grateful to share Lil's breakfast. We began chatting like old chums, willy-nilly as the random memories crowded back—the great fires—"I was cleaned out; had nothing left but my night-shirt and poll parrot." The Christmas Eve party when Pearl De Vere killed herself—"She was mad about that fellow Stratton and he turned her down." Mrs. Sam Vidler and the time she caught her husband in Room 213 at the National Hotel with Nellie Smith and shot her dead. "She should have got him, too. He was no good and they let her off under that unwritten law—"

She spoke of her life "on the row" without a trace of self-consciousness or apology. "It was a tough way to earn a livin'—dog-eat-dog mosta the time. But I had fun fightin' the other girls. Lord, it's a wonder I got any hair left the way Leo the Lion used to pull it out when I stole a guy away from her." She sat back in her chair and laughed so heartily that I joined in spontaneously and asked her to tell me more about Leo the Lion.

"She was the meanest wench that ever hit camp," Lil began. "Everybody hated her. I an' her used to battle up one side of Myers and down the other. Her hair was flaming red and she had the same kind of temper. She was always accusin' me of swipin' fellas away from her crib and often threatened to cut out my heart or split my guts. But I wan't afraid of her. I had been a big, husky farm girl back in the Midwest and could handle the worst of 'em. Years later —that was after I went over to Salida to work among the rail-roaders—Leo got herself into a pecka trouble over that story by a fella named Julian Street who made the camp out as the worst red-light district in the county. I had to laugh when folks got so mad about it. They run Leo out of town

[49]

and dubbed Myers Avenue, Julian Street, as if anybody ever cared a hell of a damn."

The coffee had grown cold and she took the pot to the kitchen to reheat it. "I just about live on the stuff," she called back, "an' always try to have a pot simmerin' on the back of the stove. I never did take to booze or cigs—sometimes a pipe maybe, but, good Lord, I've drunk a' ocean full of coffee in my time."

"How old are you, Lil?" I asked, handing her my cup for refilling.

"I'll be eighty come December, an' my joints 're not lettin' me fergit it."

"Have you any family?"

"Only a younger sister who's back East someplace." She took a sip of the steaming drink. "I've always been a loner an' that's the way it'll be until I turn up my toes an' die."

"Whatever led you into becoming a prostitute?"

"Well, my father had this farm, you see, an' nobody to work it but him an' us two girls. I was fourteen, two years older than my sister, an' he forgot most of the time that we wan't horses. Got so I couldn't take it any more. It was drudgery, day after day, an' I'm tellin' you they was long days from sunup to sundown. One mornin', I decided that instead of goin' into the field to plow, I would run away to Alton, the next town, a few miles from St. Louis. I swore to God that I'd never return an' I never did. Never wanted to see my father again or anybody else in my family.

"I got a job in a laundry an' if you think that was easy, my God! It was almost as bad as the farm an' my pay was one dollar a week. Room cost fifty cents a week—there wasn't much left for all the fancy folderols I thought I could buy when I went to the big city an' earned some real dough. I took up with a girl who worked next to me. We got to talkin' one day and I asked her how she made out on such a piddlin' wage. 'I don't,' she said. 'None of the girls do on what they pay us. Every last one of us has had to git ourselves a pimp. The quicker you do this the better off you'll be.'

"I was pretty innocent in them days an' thought maybe she meant me to find myself a husband, but I'd never had a fella—I was not good-lookin' an' the farm work had stretched my figger outa shape an' coarsened my skin. But she said she didn't mean for me to find a man for keeps. So, I went to a dance with her and her beau that very night an' she introduced me to a nice-lookin' guy an' as quick as a cat could shake its whiskers, he asked me to live with 'im an' that's the way it was.

"Pretty soon my father found out where I'd gone an' began houndin' me again to come back to the farm. You see, I was under age and he still had a holt over me. I'd heard about this new minin' camp out west in Colorado where there was a gold rush on an' I made up my mind to get enough money together an' go there an' look for work. It was a wild camp with shootin's, saloon fights, an' drunks rollin' in the gutter on Myers Avenue. It was somethin', I'm tellin' you, but you know, I kinda took to it an' decided to rent me a crib an' set myself up as a professional prostitute. I been in it ever since."

She began to chuckle as her memories quickened. "I nearly split my sides laughin', sometimes, when I think of the funny things that happened. The good folks up on the hill was always tryin' to save the souls of the whores on Myers Avenue an' up in Poverty Gulch. I recollect a nice ol' nigger preacher with a mat of gray hair, named Parson Holmes, who used to drive his mule and two-wheel cart, singin' hymns an' shoutin' prayers up an' down Bennett an' Myers every night. He'd always stop in front of Crapper Jack's across from me and preach a sermon. Everybody'd come out an' stand aroun' listenin'—hell! he put on the best show in camp! One night, some tomfool kid sneaked a look at the Bible that stood open on a crate in front of the Reveren' and saw it was upside down. So, he unhitched the mule an' gave the cart a push down the street. The Parson jumped out, mad as the devil, and shouted: 'Oh, Lord, git outta dis black skin while I give dat po' sinner a thrashin'.'"

After we had calmed down from laughing, I asked her when she left Cripple Creek.

"I fergit exactly, but it was a long while ago. I went over to Salida an' hated it. Finally I moved here to Florence an' rented this house, which was big enough so as I could have five or six call girls working for me. At last I was a madam with a parlor house of my own. A big shot. Boy, I made a lot of dough, too. It just piled up until the sheriff butted in. I'm pretty well-heeled right now, if I do say it. I don't have to take no pension from the State of Colorado. I've got enough to live on. I worked hard for it. It's all mine. This house is mine. I don't have a worry in the world."

"Tell me, Lil," I said, "did you ever fall in love with any of your customers?"

She laughed. "No, no, I never did. I had no respect for 'em. All I wanted was the gimmie, gimmie." She stretched out her hand and wiggled her fingers as if clutching for coins. "I knew the almighty dollar was the best friend I'd ever have." She suddenly stared at me with strange questioning eyes.

"What'd you say was your name when you was a kid?"

"Barbee," I said. "My father was a prospector and I was about nine years old when I went to school in that sheet-iron building. I remember seeing the women chasing each other out on the sidewalk. I recall, too, how the diamond-shaped windows were shaded until noon and I often wondered about the mysterious life that went on there which apparently was so different from that of my mother and her friends." It was evident that Lil was only half-listening to me.

"Barbee," she said. "I swear I've heard that name somewheres—it rings a bell. Oh, don't worry. It ain't your papa. Now it comes back to me," she went on. "It was a lady lawyer and every girl on the row went to her whenever they got into trouble."

"That must have been my cousin Daisy," I said, flabbergasted. She was one of the first women lawyers in the country and came out from St. Louis to hang up her shingle in Cripple Creek. My mother disapproved of her because she worked mostly among poor unfortunates on Myers Avenue. But what Daisy really did was more or less a mystery to me. I smiled in retrospect. "Tell me, Lil, what kind of troubles did you girls get into, besides pulling out each other's hair?"

"Oh, I dunno. Hell was always poppin'. Cheats owin' us money. Gamblers stealin' from us. Girls swipin' each other's rakes. But there was one I remember well. Her name was Blanche. Let's see, Blanche LeCroix. They called her "French Blanche" because she had been brought over to the United States by white slavers. She couldn't speak a word of English, but Lord, what a pretty tart she was! She had all the rounders she wanted.

"Then, what do you think? One day, she up an' had a baby! When news of that got aroun' town, the good folks on Eaton Avenue made a dead set to take it away from her. No woman on Myers Avenue, they said, should have the custody of a baby, even her very own, but Blanche fought like a fiend to keep her little girl. It was this Daisy Barbee —that's her name, now it comes to me—who took her case and argued it all through the courts. Finally the judge awarded the poor kid to its mother. But she didn't keep it long. They took it away from her for good when Blanche had a howling celebration the first night the baby was home and everybody got drunk and began to fight and yell and woke up the town until the cops came. There was nothin' more Miss Daisy could do about it. I kinda lost track of 'er when I went to Salida. French Blanche, they say, is at Midway, up on Bull Cliff—she may be dead by now—I ain't heard nothin' about 'er for a long time."

My visit lasted until I barely made the Greyhound bus to Colorado Springs. It followed a beautiful highway through the wooded hills skirting Cheyenne Mountain, emerging now and then to give distant glimpses of the vast plains rolling eastward to Kansas. There was plenty of time, as we sped along, to sit back in the comfortable seat and ponder over the things Lil and I talked about, but it was the memory of cousin Daisy that clung to my mind.

It was in the late Nineties, as I recalled it, when the letter came from her to my father, saying that she had finished law school in St. Louis the year before and had been practicing there, but that she had heard about the Cripple Creek gold rush and thought she would like to try her luck in that booming camp and perhaps she, herself, might even strike it rich.

My mother objected to Daisy's coming and crowding into our little house. We had heard disturbing rumors about her from time to time and what a problem she had been to her family. Things came to a climax apparently, when she decided to go into law, a man's profession, and brought further disgrace to her parents and sisters, it was said, by practicing almost exclusively among women of the underworld. Her family treated her as if she were an orphan and Daisy decided to go so far away that they would never hear of her again, and she settled on Cripple Creek.

My mother argued that Daisy might be a bad influence for me; she was suspicious of a woman who tried to pretend that

she was a man. "There must be a funny streak in her somewhere," she said, "and I only hope that she doesn't go down
on Myers and practice her profession among those fallen
girls." She urged my father to tell her not to come.

But in due time Daisy arrived and I shared my bed with
her. She was a large, rawboned person with a high forehead
and piercing gray eyes. My mother guessed that she was
about thirty-five years old. I was a bit in awe of her, at first,
but we soon became friends and even intimates, often exchanging confidences. She told me things about herself that
shocked me, but I promised I would never reveal a word to
my parents.

Once when we were strolling up to the Lone Pine shaft,
she talked to me for the first time about her family in St.
Louis. They were good, respectable people, she said, but
terribly stuffy and old-fashioned. She had two younger, very
beautiful sisters who never lacked for beaux. They were
always being invited to balls and receiving flowers and candies
from men who wanted to marry them. Daisy was envious and
felt that she was too unattractive ever to have a suitor and
she was sure that she would die an old maid.

Her sisters were so gay and sought-after that she came
to hate them bitterly. She resolved to show up their in-
feriority to her by doing something with her life that required brains, "something they never had." She entered the
University's Law School, much against her father's wishes.
"This brought disgrace on our name," she went on, "and my
parents threatened to disown me. Things came to a high
pitch when I finished and got my degree with honors, and
was admitted to the bar in Missouri. Then, I angered my
sisters even more when my practice was largely among out-
cast women and I became known as 'Portia of the Tenderloin'
in St. Louis."

"Are you glad you came?" I asked, thinking that she might

regret having left her mother and father, if not the hated sisters.

"Yes. I like it here very much. I have the feeling that something wonderful is going to change my life one of these fine days."

It so happened that my father had a bachelor partner in leasing, whose name was Henry Seidel. He was a little shrimp of a man. It would have taken two of him to make one woman like Daisy. His bald head was fringed with gray and his brown eyes were soft and intelligent. My father had great respect, he said, for Henry Seidel, for he had gone to some college in the East and knew more about mines than the average run of so-called engineers. He was about fifty years old and we all assumed that he would never never take a wife, but he seemed to be attracted to Daisy at once. They were a bit shy and secretive about their meetings and talks together and I noticed that Daisy seldom confided in me any more.

Then, one day she and Henry were not to be found anywhere and it developed that they had eloped on the night train for Denver and no one knew where they were heading for. It was the most astonishing thing that could have happened to my family. My mother seemed relieved and excited, even though she said she was sorry for "poor Mr. Seidel" and was annoyed at Daisy for all her disgraceful actions on Myers Avenue "associating with those dreadful unfortunates." My father was pretty mad because his tried and true partner had deserted him for a woman and he didn't think Daisy was worth the price. He treated them rather coolly when they came back from their honeymoon for a brief visit. I asked her why she had eloped instead of going home with Mr. Seidel and having a big wedding in a church. She laughed and said: "That's where I was smart, honey, I knew that if I ever let my sisters see Henry, one or the other of them would surely get him away from me."

They left Cripple Creek for Tonopah, a flourishing camp in Nevada, where Daisy started her law practice again and Henry set himself up as a consulting engineer. They seldom wrote us and we gradually lost track of them. It was not until almost fifty years later that Daisy's path and mine crossed once more. I was a newly appointed member of the staff at Whitman College, in Walla Walla, Washington, and a brief story was published in the *Union Bulletin* about my training and background. The next day, Helen Kinsinger, my secretary, said: "I believe you have a second cousin living here in town. He's a friend of mine and called to say that he had read about you in the newspaper and that he was sure you were related."

"Who is he?" I asked, in surprise. I had never been one to keep in touch with relatives and was not even certain that I had any left.

"Allen Seidel—"

"How exciting!" I exclaimed. "He must be Daisy's son— is she living in Walla Walla, too?"

"No, she's an attorney in Oregon City, over on the coast." Helen went on, "She has been a widow for many years and visits Allen and his wife every once in a while. He's in business here in town."

I telephoned at once and invited him and his wife to have lunch with me. But she had gone on a trip to Seattle and he came alone. I might have recognized him on the street because of his striking resemblance to his father, as I recalled him. He had the same slight build and dark, intelligent eyes and said that he was "on the shady side of forty—just about half my mother's age—but sometimes I feel twice as old. She's still active and energetic and considered an authority on probate law," he said proudly. "I've urged her to retire

[57]

and move over to Walla Walla where my wife and I could look out for her, but she's a stubborn independent woman and refuses to give up her little home." He looked at me with a shy kind of smile which again reminded me dimly of his father. "I hope you can go to Oregon City soon," he said, "and try to influence her."

A few days later a note came from Daisy, inviting me to spend the weekend with her. She met me at the bus station with her small car and we drove around through the lovely countryside before going to her modest home. In spite of what Allen had said about her youth and sprightliness, she had all the earmarks and afflictions of a bent aged woman. Rheumatism had lamed her and cataracts were beginning to cloud her eyes. It seemed a miracle that she was able to drive her car back and forth to the office.

I helped her prepare a light supper which we ate in the kitchen, and afterward we sat by the wood-burning stove in her living room, talking endlessly about our days together in Cripple Creek. She told me something that I had never known until that evening. She had been the fourth woman ever to take a law degree from a reputable school in the United States, she said, and the first of her sex to be admitted to the bar in the state of Missouri. "Except for the barrier it set up between me and my family, I've never regretted it. Next to Henry Seidel and my son," she went on, reaching for her handkerchief to blow her nose, "the practice of law has been the first love of my life."

Against my strongest protests, she had prepared her only bed for me. "I like to sleep on the sofa," she said, "where I can look out at the sky and see the stars." She went into the bedroom and changed into a long flannelette nightdress that buttoned up around her neck and wrists. I had already slipped into a flimsy blue sleeveless and neckless gown and was pulling off my nylon stockings. Daisy sat in her big Morris chair and watched spellbound every move I made, from rubbing the cold cream on my face to putting my hair up in pin curls.

"I should think you'd freeze to death in that silly excuse for a nightgown," she said finally. "Wouldn't you like to borrow my hug-me-tight? It gets pretty cold here at night when the fog rolls in."

I reassured her that I would be all right and laid my stockings across the back of a chair. "My goodness," she exclaimed, "how do you ever keep your legs warm in those crazy things!" I stretched a point by telling her that nylon stockings were much warmer than they looked.

It occurred to me suddenly that it would be better if I kept mum about her moving to Walla Walla. I hadn't yet met Allen's wife, but I was sure that she was young and very nice, and without doubt, addicted to nylon stockings and sheer nightgowns—trifles that could easily disrupt the family's harmony. I was aware that even Daisy and I were finding it difficult to stand on common ground or communicate. We had lived too long in separate worlds and as the years passed, we hugged our rooted habits and ways of thinking closer and closer, until we did not want the same things of life.

There were many questions I longed to ask about her memories of Cripple Creek, and especially those of French Blanche and her futile struggle to win custody of her baby. But the words wouldn't come. I feared she might not want to recall that dark phase of her career and I knew little or nothing about law courts. Perhaps, I thought, when she came to visit Allen and his wife next time, we would feel better acquainted and talking together might be easier. But I never saw her again. A few months later, word came that a neighbor, seeing no light in the little cottage one evening, opened the unlocked door and found that Daisy had died;

she was slumped down in her Morris chair with a shawl over her knees, and the fire in the stove had burned out.

I was so lost in my baffled musings about Daisy that I hardly realized the Greyhound had reached Colorado Springs and was turning up Nevada to the station on the corner, at Pike's Peak Avenue. Nate walked over, eying the arriving passengers for transfers to the Cripple Creek bus. I was the only one and his face lit up when he spotted me. "Bob Ragle said you had gone down to Florence this mornin' an' might be comin' back to the Springs on the Greyhoun'—told me to watch for you," he blurted out, "'cause you went visitin' Two-Bit Lil!"

Nate seemed wound up for a long gabble about her and all the other screwy characters he thought I should write about "in that there book." But I was too weary to pay much attention and moved toward the back before the bus filled with Ute Pass commuters. "Guess you're kinda tired," Nate said, taking the hint. "That circle trip's too much to make in one swing."

"Yes, I've had a long day—fifty years long, as a matter of fact," I said, settling down in the seat and closing my eyes.

# IV

# When We Were Young and Pretty

I returned from Florence to find signs of life in Mrs. Eads'
apartment, across the stairs from mine. "Doc Denman musta
went down to the Springs to bring 'er home," Nate said,
as he braked to a stop in front of the McMillin Building.
"She swears by 'im. Once she was on a trip and caught
pneumonia way down in Farmington, New Mexico, an' she
sent for 'im to come an' get 'er—said if she was going to
turn up her toes she wanted to be in the Doc's hospital over
in the Creek with 'im holdin' 'er han'. She's quite a gal,"
he said, pulling the bus door shut. "You'll like 'er."

The fringed shades were up and flowery chintz draperies
fluttered in the breeze of an open window. Somewhere inside a tuned-up radio was blaring a familiar song called,
"It's So Nice to Have a Man Around the House." I had to
smile at the thought that I was trapped between the deathly
silence of a mortuary down below and the earsplitting jangle

[61]

of a radio in the rooms next door. I recalled then A.W.'s comment that "although Grace is just eighty-three, already cataracts are blinding her eyes and only a clumsy kind of hearing aid saves her from total deafness. But she gets around, with the help of strong lenses," he added cheerfully, "and has a zest for life that puts us all to shame."

I was grateful to have a living, breathing, laughing human being within reach and could hardly wait to thwack the brass knocker on her door. At last I heard measured footsteps within and suddenly found myself being warmly embraced by a little old lady with touched-up auburn hair, whom I couldn't remember ever having seen before. She looked at me through her thick glasses and said that the Olivers had told her I was going to be her neighbor. "Come right in," she urged hospitably, opening the door wide, "and make yourself at home!"

It was like entering another world. She had furnished the place beautifully, as if expecting to live there the rest of her days. I had been told that Norris, her husband, had made a great deal of money in the hardware business before he died a number of years ago and since they had never had any children, she was free to indulge her taste in surroundings so pleasant and homelike that I soon became unaware of her physical handicaps.

"It must have been a tiring day," she said, when I told her about my adventure in Florence. "Sit here in this comfortable chair and relax while I mix us a couple of old-fashioneds." She went to the kitchen a few steps along a narrow corridor and soon I could hear her fussing with glasses and opening bottles. "By the way," she called back, "did Viola Oliver think to tell you to drop in on Mary Rankin while you were down there? She's an old Victorite and quite a character. Viola says she's cracked, but I'm not so sure. I'll tell you about her when I come back in."

She put the drinks down on a table and pulled a chair close to me. We needed no further preliminaries for getting acquainted. It was as if we had known each other always and had just caught up again after sixty years of separation. She was only twenty, she told me, when her family arrived in Cripple Creek with the gold rush in 1894, and she opened a small millinery store next to the Bazaar on Bennett Avenue. "I remember it all as if it were yesterday," she went on, "especially a youngster named Mabel Barbee—"

"Oh, that can't be," I protested. "I was only ten or eleven then—"

"Don't tell me what I remember!" she broke in sternly. "You used to hang around my shop after school, trying on the gay, flower-trimmed hats—you looked real pretty in them. You were so careful I was never afraid you'd soil them."

"I must have been ridiculous," I said, "for it was at about that time when my family was so poor that I often had to go barefooted and didn't have a whole pair of shoes to my name!"

"You couldn't have looked ridiculous to me," she said, adjusting her glasses. "You were a very pretty child. Your eyes were the bluest and your cheeks the pinkest—I asked you once if you ever painted them with that drugstore stuff at the Palace Pharmacy but you denied it. Said your father would have whipped you if you ever tried to fix yourself up like a hussy." She came over and put her hand on my head. "I can still see your hair, too, the color of gold with glints of red in it—I guess it's not the same now."

"No!" I laughed. "It's gray and thinning and, alas, my blue eyes have faded along with my pink cheeks. But I've never lost my weakness for bewitching hats. I probably have you to thank for this engaging bit of vanity. What was the story you said you were going to tell me about Mary Rankin?"

"Her husband, Sam, ran the Diamond Saloon that's

[63]

boarded up now over there across the street," she began. "It was a great place for miners to go after shift or to gamble away their money at night. Sam was known as a pretty tough character and once threatened to kill a fellow in a dispute. He and Mary had eight or ten rooms up over the saloon where they lived and rented some to young fellows working in the mines.

"Mary had one son by a previous marriage, and she seemed to want to mother all the boys who came into the saloon for one reason or another. Pretty soon everybody was calling her Mother Rankin. She used to do a lot for the young fellows who rented her rooms. She'd mend their clothes and sew on buttons and if the shirts weren't clean when they came from the wash, she'd scrub them over again. The Diamond Saloon was a great hangout for fellows like Lowell Thomas, where he sold newspapers and brushed elbows with tough guys like Jim Warford and Harry Orchard.

"Ralph Carr was another one of Mary's favorites. It was like a second home to him to come over and see her after he left his office. She was mighty proud of him when he was elected Governor of the state a few years later. Mary was thrifty, too, and it was said she controlled the slot-machine racket up here in the District and made a pile of money.

"When Sam died, she pulled up stakes and moved down to Florence where she bought a hardware store and lived in ten or twelve rooms upstairs over it. A friend of mine went down to see her one day and said Mary was pretty feeble and her mind seemed to wander. All the bedrooms that she didn't occupy herself had been fixed up ready for her "boys" to use any time they came back to see her. But none of them ever stopped over in Florence except Lowell Thomas and Ralph Carr. She would get their letters out of an old album and try to get everybody who called on her to read them. Pictures of Lowell and Ralph were pasted on the walls and she'd stand at the window when the bus went through from Salt Lake hoping to see someone she knew get off and rush up the stairs to see her.

"I've often thought I'd get Nate to drive me down some day and I spoke to him about it once but he said it would be a waste of time. She thinks now that her husband was a Catholic priest and that the Diamond Saloon, where he earned his living, was a Y.M.C.A. So, I decided that it would be too sad for me to make the trip to visit with Mary. Sometimes, you know," Mrs. Eads went on, "you've got to let go of your old friends when the ties that held you together have snapped."

It followed naturally, after a day spent in pouring over issues of the *Morning Times*, that Grace Eads and I should have dinner together in the evening at Mame's Café, and afterward sit for an hour or two in her cozy living room exchanging reminiscences. "What wonderful times I had," she said nostalgically, "picnicking over on Spring Creek on Sunday, or buggy riding with a beau in Box Canyon, or coasting with a crowd down Golden Avenue hill in winter, or dancing at the Klover Klub balls! And oh, the grand celebrations!

"I remember best," she continued, "one Labor Day when Danny McCarthy, superintendent at the Granite Mine, had charge of arrangements. He was a big, openhearted fellow and decided that nobody in camp should be left out of the festivities, not even the girls on the row. So he invited all of them in Cripple Creek and Victor to sit in the office windows along Bennett Avenue and view the parade. A few men objected and locked their offices. Several others skipped town suddenly, out of fear people said. When the ladies up on Eaton Avenue saw what had happened they were incensed. Danny tried to pacify them by saying that whatever the sins of their fallen sisters may have been, they wouldn't rub off on them now. But so loud was the roar of protest that it almost broke up the celebration, and Danny left town before the day was over and stayed away until tempers had cooled off." She laughed until the tears rolled down her cheeks. "Oh, that Irish Danny," she said, blowing her nose, "he was the craziest cutup in the whole District!"

"You must have been a very attractive, popular girl," I put in, "with lots of beaux. How did you happen to meet Norris Eads?"

"I forget exactly—it's been so long ago. He was working as a foreman at the Brodie Gold Reduction Mill down in Mound City, about a mile south of Cripple Creek. Not a scrap of anything is left of that camp today, but it was being boomed then as the coming metropolis of the District, chiefly I guess because it lay on the only level stretch of land in the basin.

"Norris was considered quite a catch," she went on. "He was tall and rugged and had a way with women and I fell for him in no time. It didn't take me long to get rid of my millinery store when he said he'd bought a three-room cabin for us not far from the mill. Seems to me we were married the next day by Reverend Franklin at the Baptist Church." She got up and started for the kitchen. "What do you say to a cup of coffee? I need something to wet my whistle." It was the usual break in our nightly sessions to remind me that it was almost her bedtime.

One day coming from the mill, I found an exciting letter in my mailbox. Sometime before, Lowell had suggested that I get in touch with a long-time friend of his who had roughed it in Cripple Creek in his early youth. "He might have some interesting anecdotes to tell," he added. "His name is Wallace Irwin. A note addressed simply to Southern Pines, North Carolina, would reach him. You've doubtless known of him as the famous novelist and poet as well as the brother of Will Irwin, distinguished as a newspaper reporter."

Recently I had been having arguments with old-timers concerning the weather at the time of Cripple Creek's second big fire in April of 1896. I recalled that it was bitter cold with a stinging blizzard blowing down from Pike's Peak. Grace Eads agreed with me but many others swore that it had been a balmy spring afternoon. It occurred to me that for accuracy's sake an opinion from Wallace Irwin might carry weight and settle the dispute and I used this as an excuse for writing him at once. But several weeks passed without a reply and I decided that he probably was too busy to answer idle inquiries about his flapjack days in Cripple Creek. And now this letter had come, written in longhand, giving a fascinating account of his experiences during the Great Fires, when he was an eighteen-year-old assayer's assistant at the Brodie Gold Reduction Mill in Mound City.

He was almost a decade older than I and well established as a literary personage by the time I was in college. He was best known then, not only for his *Chinatown Ballads* but for a series of humorous stories running in the *Saturday Evening Post,* called *Letters of a Japanese Schoolboy* and *Mr. Togo, Maid of All Work.* There were few people of my era who hadn't laughed periodically over Irwin's amusing tales. I felt sure that Grace Eads would remember them and perhaps she might even have known him when she was married and living in Mound City. I could hardly wait to show his letter to her that evening.

"He was a bit younger than Norris and I," she said, "but I recollect him clearly. We called him Wally and often used to have him in for supper just to hear him spout poetry. Neither of us understood a word of it but we liked his flair for dramatics and his killing sense of humor. He was a nice-looking kid, too, in a tall, gangly kind of way, and well mannered. Must've come from good people."

"Did you ever read any of his *Letters of a Japanese Schoolboy?*" I asked. "Or his poems, *Love Sonnets of a Hoodlum?*"

"I have to confess, my dear, that I completely lost track of Wally when we moved from Mound City to the Creek. Norris had quit his job at the Brodie Mill and was leasing on Bull Cliff and our lives were taken up with new folks." Then she said apologetically, "I've never been much of a reader—didn't know he became a famous author. I never went far in school because my eyes began to weaken when I was just a kid. It wasn't possible to get decent glasses then and I seldom saw anything but the headlines in newspapers, and Norris read only the mining and sports pages. What does young Irwin write in the letter?" she said, "It may take me back to my happy youth!"

Dear Mrs. Lee: (it began)
Your knowledge of Cripple Creek as it was makes me feel that I can't add anything worth a plugged nickel to what you know so well. I was in on the second fire, the rough one, but my memories are as vague as that of a nightmare which you half forget the moment you wake. From Mound City we could see the smoke streaked with flames rolling toward Mineral Hill and we decided to organize a militia, cavalry, of course. We had no uniforms, no drill, no anything. Our captain was a graduate plumber, full of pomp and gestures. A howling blizzard was raging in the hills—

"You see," I said to Grace rather pompously, "I was right about that blizzard—it was raging in the hills—Wallace Irwin says so right here—"

[68]

"Well, it don't matter now," Grace said, rather impatiently, "get on with the letter—"

A howling blizzard was raging in the hills [I repeated], when down the street charged Captain Plumber, impersonating Paul Revere. Pounding on doors, he yelled frantically, "Get a gun, get a horse—the Creek's on fire again!" I belted on the family Colt, mounted the family broncho and followed the cavalcade. When we got in sight of Cripple Creek, by now almost down to a smoulder, Captain Plumber addressed his troops. "It's firebug work—probably them Irish mossers from Victor. My orders are," he pontificated, "if you see anything suspicious shoot first and ask questions afterward!"

Grace was doubled up with laughter. "Norris couldn't ride a horse to save his life," she said. "He was more at home on a jackass. But he buckled on his gun belt and joined that bunch of crazy, half-loaded militia men. I was worried sick—"

I was in the saddle 48 hours [the letter continued], seeing nothing worth shooting at, doing nothing more practical than to pity the homeless families wandering toward anything that promised shelter. Muffled up women stood at every charred corner offering soda crackers and coffee to the heroic horsemen. The gay ladies doled out whisky, their loot from the wrecked saloons. Now and then we rounded up a suspicious looking tramp and he was glad enough to go to jail, out of the cold.

On the second night, completely woozy, I achieved the Brass Medal of Honor. Behind what had once been a grocery, I saw several sneaking figures crouched, heads together, over an inflammable litter. I dismounted stealthily, braced the family Colt against a post, fingered the trigger and was about to squeeze it but I hesitated, I'd always been afraid of that gun—it had a bad kick and never hit anything I aimed at. Suddenly one of the

[69]

crouching conspirators lit a match and puffed on a cigarette. The illumination revealed a flash of gold lace— they were all in uniform, officers of the National Guard who had come up from Denver!

We both laughed until tears came. I calmed down finally and skimmed ahead in the letter, reading to myself, but Grace reprimanded me, saying that I mustn't leave out anything; she wanted to hear every word. "He must have got hurt, somehow," I said, beginning to read aloud again. "Listen to this—"

My career as a deputy sheriff ended in an improvised hospital, in a schoolhouse somewhere. I don't know how I got there but I had to stay for a couple of weeks and then some. When I got back on my pins I served as an orderly in the strangest of hospitals. They had put stretchers over the school desks and pneumonia was rampant.

I hope you'll forgive me for any inaccuracies. I've been a tenderfoot for fifty years or more, and in the Mound City and Cripple days I was, like a jackass, more interested in Elizabethan poetry than in the fabulous literary gold among those hills . . .

"Is that all—didn't he once mention knowing Norris and me, and how he used to come to our house for supper?" Grace asked, disappointed.

"Oh, there's a lot more," I said, beginning again. "Now he tells something about the Brodie Gold Reduction Mill and his work there—"

It was a Scotch concern [he continued], and I spent most of my time shoveling coke and weighing gold buttons in the assay office. The mill extracted the gold by dumping powdered lowgrade ore into great vats and covering the mess with a weak cyanide solution. After the precious metal had fallen to the bottom of the vat the tailings were sluiced off to tumble over dreary mounds of mud in the gulch below the mill. The first novel I ever wrote was called "Venus in the East" and it ran serially in the *Saturday Evening Post*. When I wrote it I didn't know that I was being prophetic. But millers used to say, pointing at the mud, "there be gold in them mounds."

Undoubtedly a great deal of gold was wasted in the enormous discard. Therefore, I made my hero a chemist with a formula for recovering gold from tailings. Naturally, he got rich and to the best of my recollections, married the beautiful daughter of an English Duke and lived in style ever after. Well sir [he went on], not so long ago I saw in the papers where a South African metallurgist had discovered just such a formula as the one I created in my novel, and made a fabulous fortune from it.

"That was very smart of Wally," Grace commented, "go on—go on—"

The gulch leading from Mound City to Cripple Creek was reputedly infested with bandits [he wrote, changing the subject]. I never heard of any desperate holdups in that strip of wilderness. But one of life's big moments for me was on Friday morning when the mill had melted its gold into convenient size bricks. They were then canvas wrapped and put into an open buckboard. A half dozen of us, armed with carbines, rode along as a posse with Mr. Ingalls, our very-very English superintendent taking the lead. He had a little blond goatee, wore London tailored breeches and everything but a monocle. Although I'm no great hand at trading bullets with bandits, I sometimes wished that they would pour out of the bush, just to see what Mr. Ingalls would do. Would he have turned his thoroughbred's cropped tail and scooted for safety; or would he have frozen the outlaws

[71]

with one of those British stares with which he quelled
employees of the Brodie Gold Reduction Mill? I never
knew, for the precious freight was always quietly de-
livered to the mint's officials in Cripple Creek. There
were never any brigands in sight.

"I remember that Mr. Ingalls," she said, brightening. "He
was very agreeable after you got to know him. When Norris
quit the mill job and went to leasing up on Bull Cliff, we
moved to a big house on Florissant Avenue in Cripple Creek
and Mr. Ingalls sometimes came to dinner. He got over looking down his nose at people and acting superior. I guess he
considered Wallace Irwin pretty much of a kid—"

"That's just what he wrote about himself here," I said,
finding my place again:

I'm afraid all this is pretty useless to you historically
[he apologized]. I was eighteen at the time and rather
young for my age, and didn't know any of Colorado's
Empire Builders. On Saturday night, I usually went with
my partner, Bill Rich, up to Cripple Creek to wander
around the gambling halls and work out schemes to
break the bank. We tried it once, financed by two
months' salary. It didn't work so Bill went home spitting
like a cat. I wandered some more and in the lining of
my coat found my last four-bit piece.
  I stopped at a roulette table where a big mining man
was spending a pocket full of double eagles with no return for his money. An idea struck me. When he put his
money on the black I put my four bits on the red. As
he invariably lost I invariably won—until I got ambitious
and stacked my winnings on two numbers. The dealer
methodically swept in my cash with the miner's last gold
piece. Then he said, obedient to custom, "The drinks're
on the house. What'll you have Mr. Casey?" "Whisky
straight," said Mr. C. "And you?" asked the dealer with

the glance of a kindly snake. "The same," I replied, assuredly. "Do tell!" sneered the dealer. "Well—you'll have milk, you little bastard. You're under age. Git!"

About the weather during that second Cripple Creek fire. I hope the old-timers won't come down to Southern Pines and shoot me for what I said about the blizzard. I've spent so many years as a romantic novelist that I can't trust my memory which is apt to add a cyclone or an earthquake, just for effect.

With best wishes for your book, which should be a very live baby.

> Faithfully yours,
> Wallace Irwin

P. S. If you ever run across some Mound City old-timers named Eads, give them my affectionate best. Tell Mrs. Eads she made the most delicious dried-apple pies I have ever eaten, before or since!

I had been so absorbed in the letter that I had not noticed that Grace had suddenly slipped out of the room. A cork popped and glasses were tinkling in the kitchen. "This has been such a red-letter night," she said, sitting down beside me again, "I decided to open a bottle of my vintage port. What do you say if we drink a toast to the health of my old friend, Wallace Irwin!" And I noticed as she held the tawny glass up to the light that her cheeks were still damp with tears.

# V

# The Phantom Bonanza
# of Battle Mountain

Victor was just another big camp in the Cripple Creek District when I was a child, and I hadn't the remotest idea of where Battle Mountain was except as the place where two great mines, the Independence and the Portland, had been discovered. W. S. Stratton, who owned the former, was a friend of my father and came to see him now and then at our house on Golden Avenue. They were a strange pair of mavericks and argued endlessly about the rich promise of Battle Mountain as opposed to that of Beacon Hill to which my father pinned his hopes. In the end, Mr. Stratton always won.

It wasn't until I began to teach in the Victor High School, after finishing college, that I fully appreciated the magnitude of Battle Mountain's treasure. From my classroom window I had a clear view, not only of the two famous mines which

I had known before, but of many others—the Vindicator, Ajax, Golden Cycle, Findley, Granite, and the Strong pushing into the north end of town. I was fascinated by the sight of the miniature men emptying ore cars over the huge gray and ocher dumps. My eyes followed the twisting, winding trails etched by the boots of hundreds of miners. And occasionally, on Sunday afternoons, I had gone walking with Howe, a young engineer at the Vindicator Mine, who was courting me. He told me stories of some of the miraculous strikes made by such men as Jimmie Doyle of the Portland, who had once been a handyman, and his partner, Jimmie Burns, a plumber. Sam Strong, who ended in a murderous brawl over in Cripple Creek, had been a butcher and a roustabout before striking it rich. "Stratton was the smartest of them all," he said, as we were passing the commodious cottage he had built for himself a few yards from the Independence. "He was a lone wolf—never had any partners and only one enemy—liquor, and not many friends. Finally he sold his mine to the Venture Corporation of London for eleven million dollars—quite a tidy sum!"

One day as we were strolling down the mountain, we came to a rocky stretch of land about halfway between the Portland and the Independence. A few dumps here and there indicated that it had been prospected unsuccessfully in the past. A boarded-up shaft building, topped by a rickety smokestack, added to the picture of blasted hopes. "That's the Clyde property," Howe said, "one of Battle Mountain's few failures."

"A decade or so ago," he went on, telling me the story, "the Clyde was only a jagged claim consisting of scarcely more than seven acres, considerably less than what Colorado mining law required for a claim. But its location was irresistible to tenderfeet. The great Portland vein system spread only fifty or sixty yards down this slope here," he said, with a sweep of his arm, "the Findley was up the hill not faraway, and edging Victor on the other side was the Gold Coin." He pointed across the gulch eastward where I could see smoke belching from a giant black stack. "And there lies one of the greats—the Golden Cycle!"

"It seems strange," I said, "that one of the owners of those rich producers didn't acquire the property."

"They were shrewd mining men," Howe said. "For some reason, not a single Battle Mountain Croesus showed any interest in owning the claim that crowded the space in his back yard. So far as I know it was only a daydream in the minds of gullible Midwesterners."

I soon forgot about the Clyde. A year later, Howe and I were married and went to live at the Camp Bird Mine, near Ouray, in Southern Colorado's San Juan Mountains. It was not until I returned to the District after some forty-five years and began reading the old copies of the *Morning Times* stored at the Carlton Mill that I ran across news items about the Clyde Mine and its ill-fated history.

Around the turn of the century, a newcomer from Detroit began nibbling at Cripple Creek mining stocks and happened on what he apparently thought was a potential bonanza in the unwanted Clyde Mine. His name was Frank C. Andrews and as a director and vice-president of the City Savings Bank of Detroit, as well as commissioner of police, no person was more highly esteemed. Already, at the age of thirty, he was generally regarded as the city's most astute young businessman; his opinion carried weight. "The Clyde property," he wrote home to one of his friends, "lies in the heart of Battle Mountain, surrounded by gold deposits that stagger the imagination. It's a sure bet!"

He had no difficulty in organizing a company and raising cash for the purchase of the mine. It was capitalized at 1,000,000 shares of common stock with 200,000 preferred

[76]

to be kept in the treasury together with $7000 in currency as a backlog. Development began immediately with the sinking of two shafts of nine hundred feet and a lateral drift of four hundred feet. But not a trace of ore was found.

Money vanished quickly and the Clyde's reserve funds were getting dangerously low. But Andrew's optimism never ran out and since he was both president and treasurer of the company, he was free to use his own ingenuity in meeting expenses. He invested heavily on margin in Amalgamated Copper, bought several more Cripple Creek claims on a gamble, and built a mill down the hill from the Clyde and called it the Detroit Reduction Company. It was planned to treat ores, not only from the parent mine but from other District producers as well. This proved to be a costly mistake. Neither the Clyde nor any other prospects ever produced enough ore to warrant treatment.

Meanwhile, James F. Burns, co-owner of the Portland, knowing Andrews' desperate financial straits and fearing that he might be tempted to tap some of the Portland's adjacent veins, posted guards in ore chutes to make certain that Clyde miners kept within bounds. Evidently, when Andrews bought the mine, he was either unaware or unmindful of the Colorado mining law, which stated that a vein belonged to the property on which it apexed, but not one of the great lodes on Battle Mountain surfaced on Clyde land. Labyrinthine tunnels and drifts honeycombed the mountain but none of the golden arteries ever came to light on Frank Andrews' benighted piece of land. He said the law was unfair; he had no choice but to mine ore that was his by rights, no matter where the vein apexed. He sued and spent more of his dwindling funds, but the courts decided against him.

Catastrophes began to multiply. It was reported that Andrews had lost $400,000 in Amalgamated Copper. The costly mill which he had built was fast becoming a shambles, a breeding place for rats. The Clyde hadn't returned a single dollar on the investment. But Andrews' faith burned brighter than ever. If only he could get his hands on more money! Unless that could be done soon, disaster would strike. But perhaps there was still a way out . . .

He was known to be a persuasive young man with a magnetic personality. It was easy for him to convince the company officials to incorporate the Clyde and include the various other worthless properties he had bought with the deal. It was called the Detroit-Cripple Creek Gold Mining Company and a new issue of stock was voted to meet outstanding obligations.

But on January 9, 1902, Frank Andrews' brilliant coup backfired. He was charged with embezzling $600,000 from the City Savings Bank of Detroit by means of overdrafts. The victims were mainly laboring people. The Board of Education, with an account of $467,000, was the heaviest loser. It was estimated that thousands of dollars had been sunk in Andrews' fruitless search for the Clyde's supposed bonanza.

He was tried and found guilty of misappropriating $8000, which he had written with a check on the City Savings Bank payable to the National Bank of Detroit. The money had been diverted to his own personal use. At the time, he was overdrawn at the bank, of which he was a director and vice-president, to the extent of $300,000. The court sentenced him to fifteen years in the old Michigan State Prison, but he was paroled because of ill health after serving eighteen months.

Andrews died soon after his release and A. E. Carlton, an experienced hand in Cripple Creek banking and mining, bought the Clyde from the estate at sheriff's sale for $7054.81 to satisfy a judgment for mining supplies. Later the property

[78]

was sold to Frederick G. Lazier, a graduate of Michigan College of Mines. Carlton told friends that he would have been willing to get rid of it for taxes.

Lazier, too, came under the Clyde's spell. He engaged a reputable engineer to make an examination, but in spite of the discouraging report he bought forty more acres of surrounding land without a vein apexing on any one of them. A main shaft was sunk fourteen hundred feet in the hope of getting below the Portland vein system. He was convinced that he would uncover the Clyde lode at greater depth. Now and then he came upon small pockets of ore amounting altogether to about $60,000, but this scarcely paid the cost of milling. Lazier's personal fortune was almost exhausted and he was forced to close down operations. Johnny Brown, a Victor man and former superintendent, was employed as watchman.

I was captivated by the story as I skipped through the files of the *Morning Times,* looking for better news about the Clyde's fate. Then, suddenly the old papers came to an abrupt end with a half-filled volume—a holocaust had struck the camp. It was April 1917. The United States had joined the Allies in the war against Germany. Cripple Creek never recovered from the shock. The fabulous mines were soon stripped of young men either being drafted or volunteering for the Armed Services. Labor forces had become mere skeletons. No one was left to drill and blast the hard rock in the stopes and drifts, or to man the pumps against flooding underground streams, or to operate the cages and stoke the furnaces. No one, that is, except a limited number of older, often decrepit workers. To make matters worse for the mine owners, the United States Government, after the declaration of war, placed certain embargos on the export of gold from the United States. Controls were imposed by the government which made it difficult for the gold-mining industry to get priorities for equipment needed for mining and smelting operations. Many of the once great producers were closed and boarded up and leasers worked over the dumps.

In thinking back over the day when A.W. had driven me to Victor along the range road down past all the famous old mines, many of them defunct, I wondered how he forgot to tell me about the Clyde. He had once been connected with the Copeland Sampling Works not far from the Independence and must have been familiar with all that area, the dud mines as well as the rich ones. I met him on Victor Avenue one day, and we went into the Silver Dollar lunchroom for a cup of coffee. I told him of my interest in reading about the Clyde Mine and that I was curious to know if Mr. Lazier had ever done anything more with it.

"Good Lord, yes—those Detroiters were fiends for punishment! The mine buildings stood padlocked for years, and Johnny Brown made a living out of guarding them." A.W. took a few sips of coffee and settled back in his chair as if mulling over long-dormant memories. "It was in 1932, I think, when Cripple Creek had begun to show marked signs of age and exhaustion. Lazier received word one day that the Clyde's former stockholders in Detroit had held a meeting and voted to revive the Detroit-Cripple Creek Gold Mining Company.

"They offered to make him a down payment of fifty thousand dollars on an option, with an additional seventy thousand to be paid if and when the option was taken up." A.W. grinned ironically. "Lazier must have rubbed his eyes in amazement even while he jumped at the chance to make the deal. Apparently, even he, himself, had lost faith in the Clyde's much touted bonanza.

"Well, sir, the next thing we knew," A.W. continued, lighting his pipe, "G. Hall Roosevelt, brother-in-law of the newly elected President, Franklin D. Roosevelt, was sent to the District to make a thorough examination of the Clyde

[80]

property. He was assisted by a good friend of mine, Fred Jones, once Lazier's consulting engineer. Their report, while not encouraging, was agreeably optimistic. Samples of ore taken at various levels assayed fifty-six to sixty-six dollars a ton—not too bad a showing. It was recommended that the main shaft be sunk still deeper and a lateral be driven to uncover a possible deposit of ore that did not lie in the Portland's vein system. It was an honest report, hopeful but not actually convincing. The Detroit bankers, however, read more into it than was intended. The stockholders grew wildly enthusiastic at the prospect of recovering old losses and turning them into fantastic gains."

"What did Cripple Creekers say about it?" I asked. "It would have made them look pretty foolish if the Clyde turned out to be another Cresson or Doctor Jack Pot."

"Most of them were pretty skeptical when they talked, and yet nobody was willing to say that the Clyde was a hopeless bust. You know miners"—he laughed—"usually they'd take a chance right up to the last breath, which they're usually holding! And when word came that Harry Tyler, a big shot in Detroit, had been elected president, at one hundred dollars a day, hope began to build up in the District. Tyler was not only city budget director, he was also in charge of the city's Trust Fund for the policemen's and firemen's pensions. A new issue of stock was listed by Detroit brokers at eight dollars a share and plans were under way to list it on the New York Stock Exchange. But the government got wind of it and began to investigate Tyler's stock activities and the Clyde Mine operations.

"It came out that Tyler had used the City Trust Fund to the extent of three hundred and forty-nine thousand dollars in his stock manipulations." A.W. scraped the ashes from his pipe into a saucer and called for more coffee. "He was one of the slickest operators that ever hit camp," he went on. "Why, he even had the help of one of the vice-presidents in converting the cash from the Trust Fund to his own use. When the police went to his luxurious home in the suburbs to arrest him, he saw them coming, according to his wife, and ran to the basement and shot himself. His suicide note, addressed to her, denied the embezzlement. But the investigation later substantiated the charges against him. He had chosen death rather than certain prison."

"What happened to the Clyde then?" I asked, on edge.

A.W. let out one of his heartiest laughs. "Only Fred Lazier—also a friend of mine and a fine fellow—came out ahead. The first real money he had ever got out of that miserable hole in the ground was the fifty-thousand-dollar down payment on the option. It was enough to take care of him in his old age. He died a few years ago in California."

I told A.W. good-by, sent my regards to Viola, and went on to my apartment in the McMillin Building, still pondering the unimaginable tragedy of the Clyde Mine. Few tourists, I thought, driving over the breath-taking range road would have given a second glance to that jagged piece of land with its mute evidence of human wreckage. They would surely have read stories of the $60,000,000 produced by the Portland, and heard of the fantastic wealth which the Great Independence poured into the pockets of W. S. Stratton. But that insignificant patch of ground in between the two famous mines is marked only by a crumbling dump of yellow waste and dilapidated sheds. No legends are told of its wealth, no glories are sung of its fame. Nothing is left but legends of men who bartered their souls, more than a half century ago, for a bonanza that never was.

# VI

# Culture Comes
# to Cripple Creek

Most of the news in the old copies of the *Morning Times* was devoted to mining. Sports, especially prize fighting, ran a close second. Next came the column headed "City Briefs," which gave snatches of gossip that were both fascinating and frustrating. As a young girl growing up fast, I remembered pouring over these items. Even the advertisements slipped in between, such as "Mrs. A Harper's Hair Dressing Parlor. Bangs cut and oiled. Blondining a specialty," held me spellbound. They would be followed always by such tantalizing reports that "Bert Lang had been jailed for wife-beating," or "Token Tessie Dunn had killed herself with an overdose of laudanum for no apparent reason," or "W. H. Randle shot Sam Rankin in a quarrel over some faro checks. His vest was set on fire."

But there was one section of the Sunday paper that I

looked forward to all week. It was called simply "Cripple Creek Society." I often got up extra early in order to read it before my father started the fire with it in the kitchen stove. He had little use for those nobodies, he said, trying to act like swells and getting their names in the newspaper. He was annoyed with me for devouring their doings. "It will only give you false notions," he added, "and make you want to imitate such antics." Then my mother would come to the defense. "I suppose it's all right," she'd put in scornfully, "for you to read about 'Mexican Pete' knocking out Tom Sharkey, even though you'd gone to the fight the night before, and to spend your evenings drinking and gambling with your friends at Burnside's saloon. But Mabs is sixteen—she'd like to dress up and go just once to a Klover Klub ball, but you never introduce her to any nice young men in that crowd. All you can do is to take us to a Masonic banquet once a year on ladies' night." Then she'd pull herself up to full stature and say, "You might as well know it, Jons, we're both bored to tears with those dull as dishwater banquets!"

Their endless arguments began to ring in my ears again as I sifted through the fusty society pages of the *Times,* stored for posterity's edification, at the Carlton Mill. The perspective of more than a half century had cast them in a different light. It struck me in a heap one day that Cripple Creek, unlike other old mining camps in Colorado, such as Central City, Leadville, Aspen, and Ouray, had been bereft of culture. It had left no heritage of a Teller Opera House, no Carnegie Library, no Vendome or Jerome hotels to be refurbished, or charming homes of Victorian-American design to be renovated by future occupants. "The World's Greatest Gold Camp" had been poverty-stricken apparently in taste, sophistication, and intellectual ferment. The aim of most people seemed to be to make a quick fortune and get out of town, or probably move to a mansion on Wood or

[84]

Cascade avenues in Colorado Springs. For some reason, not many wanted to live for long in Cripple Creek after striking it rich. A familiar advertisement of the day read: "Wouldn't you like to hit a bonanza and live in a palace like John Campion's on Capitol Hill in Denver? See your Realtors— Tutt and Penrose!"

But bonanzas had a way of eluding the majority of Cripple Creek's hopefuls and apparently there wasn't much interest in raising the community's cultural level. Flimsy "opera houses" were put up from time to time in or near the red-light area, but they were used mainly as arenas for prize fights. Occasionally there were special events, such as high-school commencements or a one-night engagement of Primrose and Dockstader's Minstrels. Once a high-brow singer, Ellen Beach Yaw, "the California cantatrice with a range of four octaves," gave a concert at the Butte Opera House, just over the popular beer hall by that name. The place was so packed that the joists began to creak with the stamping and applause. The fire department had to bring the gala affair to an abrupt end. The audience yelled for its money back; no one knew for sure whether Ellen ever hit that fourth octave.

Grace Eads and I often laughed until tears came at the naïveté of Cripple Creek Society in the nineties. I was too young to do more than to read about it at the time, but she had been quite a belle in her day. One evening, the Olivers invited us to their house for dinner. I enjoyed going there, especially for the beautiful view from the ell porch and the steep steps going down which gave one a box seat for the panorama. It was on these very steps that Lowell Thomas had courted pretty Gertrude Oliver, his high-school classmate, and Viola said that on moonlight nights he often had to be reminded that it was ten o'clock and time to go home.

[85]

It didn't take long when we four got together for the wheels of reminiscence to start turning. What tricks a half century could play on one's memory! No two of us recalled the same events in quite the same way. A.W. stoutly denied my claim that the District lacked sophistication in the early days. "Why," he said, pushing his chair back from the table, "our social life was every bit as polished and cosmopolitan as that of New York or San Francisco. Consider the Victor Club, for instance; its luxurious rooms were over the Monarch saloon," he went on, gathering enthusiasm. "The woodwork was kept highly polished and the imported chandeliers were always gleaming. It was the gathering place for the elite of the District and membership was not easy to come by. When we gave our big dinners on the annual ladies' night, Negroes in spotless white waited on the tables and flower center pieces shipped up from Denver filled the dining room with fragrance and lent an exclusive atmosphere to the occasion.

"Or take the Thirteen Club, which occupied a whole upstairs floor of the Victor Hotel," he went on, holding us spellbound. "Women were never allowed even a glimpse of the sumptuous quarters." He took long puffs on his meerschaum pipe and gave Viola a sportive wink. "Important members, like Spencer Penrose, Charlie Tutt, Verner Z. Reed, and Henry M. Blackmer used to bring guests from both coasts to attend the big blowouts of the Thirteen Club. Tuxedos were *de rigueur* and only vintage wines were served at the banquets—"

"A.W.," Viola interrupted, with a facetious grin, "come back to earth—pull up your chair and have another pig's knuckle and a hot cup of Arbuckle's coffee!" And we all had a good laugh on A.W.

"It was the women who always had to take the back seat," Grace said, after calming down again. "I used to tell Norris that a mining camp was a man's world and only the girls on the row had any real fun."

"I disagree," Viola said. "We used to have swell times at our High Five luncheons, sewing circles, sociables, and the monthly hops at the Klover Klub up in Ruble's Hall. And I remember the lovely entertainments in the Church, when Bertha Van Norman would recite 'Xantippe' or 'Little Orphan Annie' or a quartette from the choir would sing 'Beautiful Isle of Somewhere' or when Hallie Martin danced the serpentine to the music of 'Hearts and Flowers' played by her big sister, Jennie. Everybody said that Hallie was good enough to go on the stage—"

"But how about the artistic and intellectual life of the camp?" I asked. "Weren't there any poets or painters?"

"Only one that I know of," Viola said. "She claimed to be a novelist and wrote a story called *Tongues in Trees* that almost turned the whole District upside down with fury. Her name was Mrs. Edward Laban Smith. A.W.," she said, turning to him, "maybe there's a copy of the book in that big dry-goods box in the basement. Go down tomorrow and look around. Mabel might like to read it."

But he drove out to the Carlton Mill the next day to tell me that he had searched through all the trunks and cartons in the house and couldn't find any trace of *Tongues in Trees*. However, my appetite for the novel by the District's only author had been whetted further by reading, that very morning, an item in the *Times,* published shortly before 1900, announcing the arrival of Mr. and Mrs. Edward Laban Smith with their baby daughter, Enola. The camp was in its heyday. "Mr. Smith, a lawyer from the East," so the story ran, "planned to open an office in Cripple Creek. Mrs. Smith was formerly on the staff of Vale College in Libertyville, Kansas, of which she is a graduate. She is also a renowned author and says that she plans to write a novel about life in 'The World's Greatest Gold Camp.'"

I showed the piece to A.W. and asked if he remembered Mr. Smith. "Vaguely," he replied. "He was a retiring sort of person, pretty much overshadowed by his wife. She was a rather handsome, aggressive woman, and managed somehow to get the old man elected to the School Board and within a year he became chairman. The ladies in town were quick to invite Mrs. Smith to join their card clubs and sewing circles but she said no—didn't like to waste her time that way. But everybody went to call on her, just the same— you know how friendly mining folks are," he said. "They go all out to make the newcomer feel welcome. Never ask where you came from or what you did for a living or how much money you had. It's what you are that counts." He picked a white thread from his coat sleeve and adjusted the yellow and purple pansy in his buttonhole as if hesitating to go on. "I gathered from Viola," he said with a little smile, "that nobody liked Mrs. Smith. Claimed she was an intellectual snob. But you know how women are—touchy—"

"What an odd name to have given their little girl," I put in. "Enola—I've never heard it before."

"Write it backwards"—A.W. grinned, turning to go—"and it spells 'Alone.'"

Now I was more curious than ever to read Mrs. Smith's novel. Perhaps it would reveal much of interest about her life. I wrote the Denver Public Library at once to inquire about the book. Fortunately a copy was found in the Western collection. It had been published in 1902 by the H. R. Mitchner Printing Press in Cripple Creek and had become a "collector's item." I was told, however, that I could borrow it, under the circumstances, for a limited period of two weeks. When I unwrapped it and saw the faded brown cloth cover, and fingered through the brittle pages, I felt as if I had discovered a nugget as rich as any ever found on Battle Mountain.

But as I began to read, disappointment mounted. It was a long drawn-out fable told by a few gossipy trees and shrubs which bordered the pink sandstone mansion called "The Ledge" owned by Judge Woodburn, the discoverer of the "Scotch Thistle Mine" on Rhyolite Mountain. The benevolent patriarch of this arboreal drama attained his high post through seniority. He was an Oregon pine of noble lineage. His lordly trunk rose two hundred feet high in the air "and flung out full plumes of foliage which dappled the shade on the saxifrage at its roots." A strong wind, it seems, had blown from the Pacific Coast many years ago and borne the little pine seedling in its embrace.

He was surrounded by other tree subjects and minor shrubs such as sage, spiraea, and kinnikinnick, and he had educated all of them to speak and understand faultless English. His own vocabulary was remarkable and such words as "shrive," "licenciate," "tergiversation" baffled my untutored brain as I read, and sent me to the dictionary. The Oregon pine, often referred to as O.P., was also a great name-dropper—Ximenes, Plato, Washington, Jefferson, Adams, Mendelssohn, Offenbach, Wagner, Zeno. And he was something of a philosopher. "Women walk their little journey through life," he said, "with gyves (shackles) on them." Once he pontificated about the cognate element of men's lives being composed of four parts—comedy, tragedy, life, and death. It didn't quite make sense to me, a human reader, but the cypress and balsam trees apparently understood what O.P. meant, for they listened intently to his every word. And now and then, he struck an impressive note by quoting in French, such as: "*Honi soit qui mal y pense!*" which would bring sighs of admiration from the dwarf juniper.

What troubled O.P. and his coniferous friends was the

[89]

spectacle of Judge Woodburn and his family, with one exception, going to the dogs because of too much money from the "Thistle." The Judge, himself, used his position for iniquitous ends. He even bragged that someday he would control every bonanza on Rhyolite Mountain and then for good measure run for a seat in the United States Senate. His wife wasn't of much help. Her purpose in life was to find a rich husband for her beautiful, virtuous daughter, Mary. But son John was the worst of all. O.P. said that he had been born a "moral cripple" and had become a hopeless alcoholic. Mary, who would have nothing to do with her mother's connivings, swore that she would devote herself forever to caring for her tragic brother, and try to save him from a drunkard's grave.

A motley group of men and women enjoyed the hospitality of the pink sandstone mansion—philanderers after Mary's favors; unfaithful wives, planning to elope to San Francisco or New York; a well-known real estate dealer making love to the Judge's wife; Eastern promoters conspiring to get control of the "Scotch Thistle"; an unscrupulous mother scheming a marriage between her beautiful reluctant daughter and a no-account butcher who had recently struck it rich, and many other despicable characters. The O.P. and his arboreal friends knew everything, heard everything, and longed to prevent the inevitable disasters, but all they could do was to talk things over, hoping, doubtless, that someday an author would write the dreadful story and put it all down in black and white in a book.

The O.P. was an extremely resourceful fellow. Naturally, none of the trees in the forest could go traveling with the Woodburns. But he made satisfactory arrangements with the many small pillows Mary had sewn and filled with ground-up cones and balsam needles. Wherever the family went, a fragrant pillow was taken along as a preventive against sickness. Actually, they sent back daily messages by the gentle south wind to keep O.P. informed as to happenings in the family. Nothing was ever missed by that omniscient old monarch!

But sooner or later, the father and mother died, and not long afterward, John, too, went to his final peace. This left Mary alone in the pink sandstone mansion, with the "Scotch Thistle" still pouring its burden of wealth into her coffers. Then she remembered the secret lover the Judge and his wife had scorned because he was poor and had no chance of getting ahead in the world. She had heard that he was connected with some important post in the State Department and she decided to go to Washington and perhaps see him again. She went with friends to the theater one night, to see John Drew in *Rosemary,* and there across the proscenium she caught sight of handsome John Caruth, her girlhood sweetheart, in a Senator's box. They met afterward for refreshments at the Mayflower and the next thing O.P. heard, there was to be a honeymoon at "The Ledge."

He called all the other trees and shrubs and even the south wind to audience and said, "I knew it had to come to pass before any of you had dreamed of it. The evening they arrived they alighted from the carriage on the road below and came first to see me. That was in keeping with the delicacy of feeling for I nourished their passion when it was in infancy. I called to the wind at that moment and it played a heavenly harp above their heads. Even sedate old Mother Rhyolite gave a tremor of joy."

"Are they happy?" asked the juniper.

"You wouldn't have known the rays of heaven had reached them except for the light in their eyes," sang the O.P. "Hear the bells ring, hear the bells ring!

"The pentstemon is saying, 'Long Life!'

"And the harebell, 'Joy, Joy!'

[91]

"And the gilia, 'Abide!'

"And I say, the peace of God be with you, my children, for the storms of life spare not even the pure in heart, the brave in spirit, or the noble of souls. And the O.P. flung up his proud head and beat the air of heaven with his fragrant arms!"

I could almost hear the harebells ringing and see the venerable O.P. waving his cones and plumes in the graceful swing of the south wind. Not since Judge Woodburn discovered the "Scotch Thistle" had there been such clean merry-making on Rhyolite Mountain, and the inspiration of it all was the happy marriage of lovely Mary Woodburn and handsome John Caruth.

I, too, had been caught up in the spirit and when the Olivers stopped by in the afternoon to invite me to a picnic on Sunday, I had to tell them about getting the book from the Denver Public Library. "You must look again for your own copy," I said to Viola. "The Librarian described it as a 'literary curiosity' and a 'collector's item.'"

"Well, do tell!" A.W. said amusedly. "I used to think the women folks who got so mad about it were making a tempest in an ink bottle."

"Maybe so. It doesn't seem so dreadful after all these years," Viola said, "but she had no right to disguise her characters so thinly that everybody knew exactly who they were—some of the District's most prominent citizens. It's a wonder some of them didn't sue her for libel."

"She got around that by putting tongues in trees," A.W. said, grinning at me. "Who ever heard of bringing a libel suit against a bunch of pines, junipers, and cypresses? Besides, all mining camps have their share of alcoholics, adulterers, and high-graders, to say nothing of crooked marshals and judges. Cripple Creek was comparatively pure except for the tenderloin and a few occasional murders. On the whole, Mrs.

Smith's novel might be considered highly moral, that is, in my lowly opinion."

I laughed. "You sound for all the world like the Oregon pine when he called all the other trees of the forest 'to audience.'"

"If that book was so chaste and free of blame, A.W.," Viola put in, with a trace of resentment, "why did all the teachers in the District threaten to quit their jobs when the Chairman of the School Board ordered them to buy it? She turned to me with a wide sudden smile, as if inspired by a great idea. "Did you say the Librarian spoke of it as a 'collector's item—a literary curiosity'?"

"I think that's the way she put it."

"Well, A.W., if this is the case, you'd better go down to the basement again and search thoroughly among our books in the dry-goods box. The grandchildren might like to keep *Tongues in Trees* as a memento of Cripple Creek's first and last brush with the literary world."

But no one can tell how far a little spark of culture will cast its flickering beam. It was several years later, long after the Smiths had faded away, that I came upon an item on the society page of the *Sunday Times* that caught my eye. It was the announcement of a new organization, called the Cripple Creek Fortnightly Literary Society. The officers were Mrs. E. C. Stimson, president and Mrs. C. G. Moore, Secretary and Treasurer. The cultural purposes and aims of the Society were emphasized and it was explained that the motto:

And this our life exempt from public haunt
Finds tongues in trees, books in the running brooks,
Sermons in stones and good in every thing.
 (*Shakespeare: As You Like It, Act II, Scene 1*)

was taken from the inscription on the flyleaf of the novel by Mrs. Edward Laban Smith.

# VII

# The Old Homestead
## at Last

I had settled into an agreeable routine during my weeks in Victor. I caught Nate's bus every morning at the Hackley Hotel corner, got off fifteen minutes later at the Carlton Mill, chatted genially with Bob Ragle as he desposited two or three heavy volumes of newspaper files on my desk, for the day's reading; and drove back to my apartment in the afternoon with one of the millworkers. As usual, Grace Eads and I had dinner at Mame's Café, and then went to her living room for a merry evening of funny stories about the foibles and scandals which I had culled from the yellowed society pages of the *Morning Times*.

It was an interesting, oddly satisfying life for me. I was not in my apartment long enough any more to be depressed by its drabness. I had even got used to the chilling quiet of the McMillin Mortuary downstairs, and seldom tortured myself, as I had done at first, reading obituary notices in the

*Gold Rush,* Cripple Creek's current weekly newspaper, antic-
ipating the number of dead who might tarry that night in the
camp's only undertaking parlor.

So it came as a kind of shock when Bob Ragle greeted
me one morning with the news that he and his wife were
going to move over to the Old Homestead at the end of
the week. "It's going to be real nice," he said, apparently
unaware of my lack of enthusiasm. "The whole place, upstairs and down, has been done over and refurbished. Nothing
of its brothel-like years remains except the elegant, green
embossed wallpaper in the banquet hall. They say that Pearl
De Vere, herself, ordered it from Europe just after the great
fires." He arranged the tomes in a neat pile and wiped the
dust from his hands on his corduroys. "The room upstairs,
toward the back, that Mrs. Ragle fixed up for you looks
fine. We found an old-fashioned brass bed with a lace spread
and pillow shams, right out of the nineties. Wouldn't be
surprised if Pearl had slept there." I forced a smile and
started to read one of the newspapers. "You still want it,
don't you?" he said quizzically, and then added, "We won't
have any trouble renting it—in case you've changed your
mind."

"How would I get back and forth to the Carlton Mill?"
I parried.

"That's no problem—you can go and come with me," he
said, "and there are one or two fair eating places up on
Bennett Avenue if prices at the Imperial are too steep for
you."

No one could have made me feel more welcome. I was
annoyed at myself for even hesitating. But it was not the
move to Cripple Creek that bothered me so much as it
was the dread of breaking the news to Grace. She was a
gallant person, but I had sensed under her cover of humor
and gaiety the unmistakable ache of loneliness. It seemed

callous of me to abandon her so abruptly to that solitary abode in the McMillin Building. But apparently I had exaggerated the importance of my companionship. She brightened when I told her that I was thinking of taking a room with the Ragles in a few days over at the Old Homestead. "That's wonderful! Of course, I'll miss you a lot," she said. "I haven't laughed so much in a coon's age. But we'll see each other often, visiting now and then, and picnicking with the Olivers." She sat back in the chair, adjusted her thick lenses, and reached for a cigarette. It was the first time I had ever seen her smoke. She explained that she had given up the habit once when Cam (Dr. A. Campbell Denman) advised that it was bad for her heart. "But occasionally, when the mood strikes me, I find food for my thoughts in a good smoke. There are several salty old-timers left over in Cripple Creek. But they are dying off fast—you'll have to hurry if you want to talk with them. Ask Viola to introduce you to George Coplen—he's the custodian at the County Court House. Once, back in 1915, he was the District's white hope for the World's Heavyweight Championship. Get him to tell you about his fight with Jack Dempsey. He doesn't like to recall it, but maybe he'll do it for you."

By the time she had finished recounting all the interesting folks I should look up over "in the Creek," I was eager to pack my suitcases and pull up stakes from Victor and head for the Old Homestead.

My mind was in such a dizzy whirl of recollections that I could hardly close my eyes the first night at the Old Homestead. It seemed incredible that after more than fifty years, I should land in the mysterious parlor house that had once stirred my childhood curiosity as I passed it on my way to and from school. I could see auburn-haired Pearl De Vere again, in fantasy, the most beautiful of all the camp's notorious madams, on whom I had a secret crush. How elegant she looked in her plaid taffeta dress and green picture hat with the sweeping willow plumes, driving in a shiny rig behind the Welty Livery's frisky, black thoroughbreds—the self-same steeds that had to be shot, not long afterward, when they broke their legs in a wild runaway down Tenderfoot Hill that killed both Alonzo Welty and his wife.

Ghosts of the past crowded in upon me. The town gossip about the night Pearl killed herself at the festive Christmas Eve ball, the day I saw her, so sweet and innocent, laid out in a lavender coffin, at Fairley Bros. Undertaking Parlor, and overheard her sister from the Midwest disown her and "wash my hands of the funeral." And I could see the long cortege when Cripple Creekers gave "the little girl the finest burial that money could buy" and Maggie Burns (Ackelbein), my schoolmate, and I wept as we watched it at the corner by Roberts' Grocery.

Far in the night, suddenly, I fancied that I heard strains of a stringed orchestra, playing "Let Me Call You Sweetheart" and soft laughter seemed to float up the stairs from the banquet hall, bringing whiffs of gardenias and rich cigar smoke. The old fear of death gripped me all at once, and I yanked the covers over my head to smother the haunting memories, and at last fell asleep.

I decided the next morning not to resume reading the *Times* at the Mill, until I had explored Cripple Creek a bit more. So many of the former landmarks familiar to me had been torn down or burned up that sometimes I had found it difficult to orient myself in the shrunken camp. I walked up and down streets once alive with children coasting or playing "kick the can," or hopscotch. Now for the most part they were only wind-swept roads. Except for a sturdy dwelling or a brick church, here and there, the weather-worn houses had been demolished and the lumber carted away. More and more, the camp had huddled in the basin, with occasional reaches toward the County Poor Farm or the Hospital on Church Hill or along the paved highway curving down Tenderfoot Hill through Old Town.

Often I took long walks over the weed-grown trails where I had tramped as a child with my father down to Mound City, now largely washed away by years of spring floods that had eroded the banks of a piddling streamlet known as Cripple Creek. Or I wandered north past the Long Pine shaft on Mineral Hill and sat for a while, gazing out at the snow-capped Sangre de Cristo or below on the remnant camp where I had been thrilled so many times by the sight of my secret idol, Joe Moore, bartender at Tom Lorimer's saloon, and leader of the Elks' Band in Fourth of July and Labor Day parades.

These and many other strolls transported me back to Cripple Creek's early days even more effectually than reading the old newspapers. Frequently, if I happened to be in the neighborhood of the County Court House, I would stop by for a chat with Viola Oliver, who never seemed too busy to gossip with me and fill in my lapses of memory. One day while we were visiting, a tall giant of a man came to her desk to report something about a leaky pipe in the basement. He was about to leave when Viola called him back. "Come here, George," she said, "I want you to meet an old friend of mine. You may remember Miss Barbee who used to teach in the Victor High School." George blushed and it was evident that he hadn't any recollection of me.

"Don't tell me this is George Coplen!" I said, trying to ease the situation. "I have been reading about your great days as a prize fighter in the District and how you just about finished off Jack Dempsey in 1915. You are almost a dead ringer for pictures I've seen of him, even today!" He smiled in a pleased, boyish kind of way, and twisted his hat around in his huge fists. "You have the same kind of broad shoulders and long arms—and must be about the same age—"

"But George is a blond," put in Viola, "and much better-looking than Jack. You ought to tell her about that fight," she added, turning to him. "By all odds you should have won it. And just think, instead of living with your ninety-three-year-old mother in that cold-water flat upstairs in the Welty Block, you might be settled with a beautiful movie star in a Beverly Hills mansion!"

I could see that George, at best, was an inarticulate, modest fellow. It would take time and tact to get him to talk about his sad encounter with young Jack Dempsey. My only hope was to get away from Viola's prompting. So, it was arranged that I would call on him and his mother the following Sunday afternoon. Ever since his father's death many years before, George and his aged Russian-born mother had occupied the three or four rooms on the second-floor corner of the Welty Block. There had been neither furnace heat nor electricity for a long time, but the old lady could find plenty to amuse her nowadays by sitting at the big front window and watching the summer tourists ambling up and down Bennett Avenue. She seldom had company, George said, because she understood very little English and spoke even less. "The only time she ever went away from the Creek," he went on, "was back in 1895 when I was about seven years old. Her and Pa took turns pushing and dragging me up the steep trail over Bull Hill and four miles down the other side to see a bullfight in Gillett."

Suddenly she began to laugh until the easy tears trickled from her eyes. "She knows this story by heart," George explained, "and I always have to tell it whenever we have company. The funny part is that they never did see the bullfight because after all that lugging, cussing, and sweating, they couldn't buy tickets—somebody in that big mob had

[99]

swiped Pa's moneybag. So they started the trip back home," he added, chortling, "and never knew 'til the next day that the gates had been padlocked by the sheriff, and Joe Wolfe and Charlie Meadows, the promoters, had landed in the pokey for trying to pull off a bullfight against the law."

I had heard and read the story of the "only bullfight ever staged in the U.S.A." many times and always in different versions, depending on the histrionic ability of the narrator or writer. I even remembered vaguely, as a child of eleven, begging my father to let me drive over to Gillett with Minnie Welty and her parents on the day of the wild spectacle. But he put his foot down against such risky business. "Bullfights 're for Mexicans," he said, in a disparaging tone, "not for civilized folks. Wolfe and Meadows 're heading for trouble—breaking the law of the land. It's no place for women and children." But now, several decades later, I had little interest in George's repetition of the threadbare tale. I preferred, instead, to get him started on his experiences as a young boxer in Cripple Creek.

He seemed to have picked up a fair education in his sixty-three years of knocking around the District and I found him intelligent and eager to talk. I commented on the three books that lay prominently on the table by a window: *Fighting for Fun* by Eddie Eagan, *In the Ring and Out* by Jack Johnson, and the *Memoirs of Jack Dempsey*. He said he had often sparred with Jack Johnson, who worked as a roustabout in a dive up in Poverty Gulch. "He had a tough time making a go as a fighter, here in camp, because he was a darky—nobody wanted to soil his fists fighting a black man."

"How did you happen to get into the game?" I asked. "Was it because of your weight, or height, or the size of your fists?"

"A little bit of all of 'em," he said. "They used to tell me, when I worked around the mines, that I was built like John L. Sullivan and ought to go in for pugilism. Pretty soon I began to take 'em seriously, and never missed a chance to scrap with the local boys." He tipped his chair back against the wall and crossed his legs and lit a cigarette. "My first real fight almost ended in catastrophe," he snorted. "Huge hulk of a pug, named Charlie Warner, came to camp expecting to put on a four-round bout. The guy who had been picked to uphold the honor of Cripple Creek—I forget his name—took one look at Charlie and backed out. The sports around town got together and said I had to box Warner, but when I saw his biceps, I tried to squirm out of the deal, said I'd never been in a real match before and didn't have any trunks.

"A geezer who had done some featherweight fighting offered me his pair," George continued, "but they looked mighty skimpy to me, and I objected. Then, the backers promised me fifteen bucks if I lasted all four rounds. That was big money in those days and I shook hands and signed a contract." He blew a reminiscent smoke ring and grinned. "I'll never forget those breeches as long as I live! They were pale blue and so tight they cut rings around my belly and legs. I swear, I could hardly breathe and was ready to throw in the sponge before the end of the first round.

"But the thought of all that wampum was like a kick in the seat and I started with the bell on second. All of a sudden, I felt an unmistakable rip somewhere in the groin and then cool air trickled in and the trunks began to feel looser. I was petrified with fear, knowing that in a minute or two I would be stark naked before that howling mob at the Lyric Opera House. Some fellow yelled, 'Knock 'im out, George, an' the fight'll be over!' So I pounded Warner with a right to the chin and a left to the eye and knocked 'im flatter than a hot cake. It was over, all right, but Charlie

Warner got the decision because I had contracted for four rounds and the fight had lasted only two. He also pocketed the fifteen bucks! I was glad enough just to get back into my pants."

George's mother and I laughed heartily at his plight. This, too, must have been one of the stories she had learned by heart. "It was lucky for me," he said, filling a dipper with water, "that it wasn't the night I fought Morgan Williams for a go of twenty rounds. Because it was billed for the Victor Opera House, women were allowed to come. Usually they were taboo—men never wanted them around the ring—said they brought bad luck," he explained. "Signs had been nailed up all over the place, cautioning the boys against 'smoking, swearing, or indulging in boisterous guffaws' in the presence of ladies. It made the fans mad as the devil and a bunch of 'em went up to Sam Rankin's Diamond Saloon on Second Street and got loaded. Then they began to lurch back to the fight, cursing and thumbing their noses at the management. I sure wouldn't have wanted Ma to be there!" He looked at her and smiled. She was sound asleep in her rocking chair, and when he saw that her shawl had slipped off her knees he went over and gently replaced it. "That Williams fight was an awful flop," he said, putting a shovel of coal in the kitchen range before sitting down again. "I rolled with a bloody right to my nose, in the middle of the second round and never heard the referee count ten!"

"I read a great deal in the old newspapers over at the Mill about all the well-known pugilists who gravitated to the District in the early 1900s," I said, anxious to draw him out further. "You probably knew some of them."

"I was too young to know such fellows as Bob Fitzsimmons, Tom Sharkey, and 'Fireman' Jim Flynn, but I used to hang around the barbershops and look at their pictures in the *Police Gazette* and wish I could grow up to be a fighter. I almost made it once, in 1915—"

"You mean the time you and Jack Dempsey had that match?" I asked eagerly. "Tell me about it, please—I'd rather hear it from you any day than go scrounging through the Cripple Creek *Times* for the story. It must have been very funny—"

Suddenly I realized that I had said the wrong thing and stirred an ugly memory. George sat for a moment, staring down at the floor, and when he looked up he smiled in a shy, embarrassed way and said: "I've got to beg off with this one. It was Jack Dempsey's eighth fight and turned out to be my last. Ask him to tell you about it sometime when you go back to California—he's there a lot with his two daughters in Santa Monica." He got up and shook the ashes in the grate and put some fresh water in the coffeepot. "There was another bout in 1915," he went on, "a few weeks before the Dempsey-Coplen fizzle and far more exciting. Maybe A.W. has already told you all about it because it was between Victor's Golden Boy, Lum Myberg, and a sixteen-year-old high-school youngster from up in Longmont, named Eddie Eagan. The kid had been causing a lot of gossip in sports circles about what the reporters called his fistic prowess, and when he won a decision over Lum Myberg, a seasoned miner from the District, at the Jacob's Club in Denver, he became welterweight champion of the Denver Athletic Club.

"But the folks over in Victor belittled the victory," George continued. "They suspected trickery somewhere along the line. Resentment in the District was sharpened by the fact that a lot of money had been lost on Myberg. One day a piece came out in the Victor *Record* accusing Eagan of being satisfied to rest on his questionable laurels and claiming that he was afraid to accept a return match with Myberg. "Well, sir," George said, giving his leg a slap, "that young colt from Longmont had a lotta guts. He let it be known on all the newspaper sports pages that he would be glad to meet Lum Myberg any time, any place, and under any circumstances, so a match was scheduled for a miners' convention to be held in Victor in early June."

"I guess it never occurred to Eagan that it would be tough fighting Lum on home grounds." George chuckled to himself. "You know Victor's nearly two miles high. Even a bloke who lives here all the time often finds it hard to get his breath if he walks fast or exerts himself too much. He can get dizzy, or sick at his stomach, or might have a nosebleed." All of a sudden, George reached on the table for Eddie Eagan's autobiography, *Fighting for Fun*, opened it on a well-worn page, and handed it to me. "Here," he said, "you can read it out loud better than I can tell it and meanwhile I'll help Ma fix us some coffee and cookies."

I glanced at the pages quickly, hoping to speak dramatically enough to impress George's mother. "My brother, John, who was my second, and I arrived two days ahead of time," the account began, "in order to get used to the altitude. The miners agreed to pay our room and board—the amateur's limit. A big crowd met us at the station. I was a bit unsteady on my feet, due to the altitude, and the welcoming committee said a drink would fix me up. So we all went over to the Gold Coin Club. I had never leaned on a bar before but knew that I was expected to order whisky or beer, so I called for a *root* beer.

"The crowd mumbled and snickered and stood around sizing up my weight and feeling my muscles. 'He's just a kid,' I heard one of them say, 'he's too light—it won't be a fight, it'll be murder!' My brother and I were bedded down at the fire station, along with the firemen. Alarms went off, it seemed to me, every few minutes during the night. I began to think it was a put-up trick. Nobody slept, not even the firemen. The street outside was jammed with Myberg fans calling out bets and cursing when there were no takers. For a few moments I felt qualmish and tried to figure a way out, but John guessed what was on my mind and he brought me to my senses with a sharp jab in the ribs. 'There's no escape,' he whispered, 'just fight that big bruiser for all you're worth—knock the hell out of 'im!'

"The Victor Opera House was a sellout the next night. I stared into a sea of hard-bitten faces. Lum was a fellow miner who had been robbed of the decision and his rightful title by a young upstart, they seemed to say, and now the time for vengeance was at hand and the whole District had turned out to see that justice was done—"

"I was in a ringside seat for the big event," George interrupted, "and the uproar was so deafening—it was a wonder the roof didn't fall in when Lum slipped through the ropes, acting very brisk and confident. I remember how the cold shivers ran up and down my spine."

"The bell clanged," I began, taking up Eddie's story again. "Myberg came at me like a Kansas cyclone. I sent a left to the nose. He charged again. Blood trickled down his chin. I drove another left to the nose, followed by a vicious right to the solar plexus. Lum grunted and wore a fierce scowl as if to intimidate me, but I was wary. He tried to entice me into his fatal right—but I was prepared.

"In the fifth round he was beginning to look spent. I sailed in, uppercutting his jaw and stomach. Lum was waiting—he almost got me with a right to my cheek. Then I heard the sweet sound of the bell. The last round had that auditorium in hysterics with yelling, screaming, shouting as the fans again saw their money going down the drain. It was terrible, but miraculously, my head was clear. Myberg took all I had—he was a tough fighter, but too slow. Finally he drooped, struggled and drooped again. It was all over.

My ears were cocked for the referee's decision. Then, he walked toward me, seized my hand and held it aloft. I was still the amateur lightweight champion of the Denver Athletic Club. But Lum Myberg was a fine sport and a great loser!"

"I was there, as I said, and saw it all," George added. "I'll never forget the pandemonium. Nobody could believe that the District's Golden Boy had lost to a kid from the plains, barely out of knee breeches, and with all the odds against him. Right away he was swamped with offers from backers and promoters, urging him to quit school and make a pile of dough as a pro. But Eddie had too much sense for 'em. He stuck to his plan of entering college in September and declared he'd never give up his standing as an amateur boxer. Kept his word, too—all the way. Not so many years later, he became an Olympic star and the amateur heavyweight champion of the world. When he finished his law course, he joined a big corporation in New York City and finally made it as a partner. One day, Cripple Creekers got the news that Eddie Eagan, the miracle kid from Longmont, who had punched Lum Myberg to the count, had been appointed Commissioner of Boxing for New York State."

"What a story!" I said, drinking the last of my coffee. "All it lacks is the tag line that he married a rich girl of fine family and has lived happily ever afterward."

"You said a mouthful!" George laughed. "That's exactly what happened. Some folks seem to have all the luck!"

I put *Fighting for Fun* back on the table, thanked Mrs. Coplen for the delicious cookies, and started to go. "By the way, George," I said, "you have a very good command of English. Has it ever occurred to you to write your own recollections as a fighter in 'the fightin'est burg in the U.S.A.'?"

He threw back his head and roared. "Why," he said, "it would take all the ghost writers in the country to make a good story out of me as a pugilist. I'm not honestly a fighter at heart. I'm better at taking care of people, like my ma here and the folks up at the County Court House. Someday when I retire as custodian, I'll get a nice pension and that'll suit me just fine."

There was a certain intelligent humility about George Coplen that had made him a perennial hero to Cripple Creekers, who still couldn't understand how Jack Dempsey could have knocked him down seven times in seven rounds and ruined his career as the camp's chief contender and "white hope" for the heavyweight championship of the world.

# VIII

# An Afternoon with
# Tom "Sailor Boy" Sharkey

I often wrote Lowell any unusual news or information that came from my talks with old-timers. Sometimes he would telephone or send suggestions in reply that led to other paths of exploration and brought fascinating people into my life. I could hardly wait to tell him about my lively afternoon with George Coplen, and how, when I asked him about his hassle with Jack Dempsey, he squirmed out of it and said I'd better get it straight from the champion himself, when I returned to California.

I also mentioned Tom "Sailor Boy" Sharkey who, according to George, was very sick at the City and County Hospital in San Francisco, "and at age seventy-nine probably wouldn't last much longer." I expressed the hope in my letter to Lowell that by some stroke of luck Tom might live long enough for me to see him on my return home in

September. "I remembered," I wrote, "that my father once lost a lot of money on him in a bout with 'Mexican Pete.' It was charged that he fouled Pete with a blow to the groin and the angry fans ran Sharkey out of camp. It would be interesting to get Tom's side of the story," I added, "while there's time."

I was constantly aware of a sense of urgency in my quest of early-day Cripple Creekers. It was as if I were racing with death. Many familiar characters were passing from the scene; men such as Jimmie Doyle, one of the discoverers of the fabulous Portland Mine on Battle Mountain and once Mayor of Victor; Fred Stone, the actor-hoofer who turned to boxing for a living when he became stranded in camp with a show called *Sallie and Oscar Kern's Comedians;* James J. "Big Jim" Jeffries, who knocked out Bob Fitzsimmons for the heavyweight crown in 1902. Their names and others were on my list of canceled appointments as having died recently, or as lying too sick in a hospital to see me. And now Tom "Sailor Boy" Sharkey, one of the most colorful and flashy of all the pugilists who ever fought in Cripple Creek, was slipping gradually into the grave, and I was helpless to reach him—or so I thought, until Lowell telephoned me from New York two evenings later, while I was having dinner with friends at the Imperial Hotel.

The point of his call was that I should consider taking several days off and go, as soon as possible, to San Francisco for an interview with Tom Sharkey. "I'll send word to my friend, Jack McDonald, sports editor on the *Call-Bulletin,* to arrange for your visit at the hospital. You'd better give him a ring when you arrive. And while you are on the coast," he added authoritatively, "it might be a good idea to fly down to North Hollywood for a couple of days, say hello to Barbara, and try to get an appointment with Jack Dempsey. I understand he's in Santa Monica just now, seeing his two daughters. I'll wire him tonight and give him your address. So long and good luck!"

In spite of the chance to see my own daughter, and the opportunity to talk with Tom Sharkey and perhaps Jack Dempsey, I hesitated for a moment about interrupting even briefly the work I had planned for my last weeks in Cripple Creek. But Lowell's advice was always paramount for me, and before realizing it, I found myself seated in an airplane, winging over the Rockies to San Francisco. I went to the Clift Hotel and immediately telephoned Jack McDonald. He said he had arranged for my call on Sharkey and that he would drive me out to the City and County Hospital early the next afternoon. He spoke of his high regard for Lowell and said that Sharkey, too, was one of "Tommie's" loyal fans—never missed his newscasts. "I usually get out to check on him two or three times a week," he went on, "and we gas a bit about the good old days when he barely missed being world champion." He pulled up at the hospital entrance and stopped. "I have an appointment shortly," he said, glancing at his watch and helping me out, "so I won't go in with you now, but 'Sailor Boy' robed, I bet, in his best emerald-green outfit will be expecting you!"

I stood for a moment at the door of an enormous ward, looking across at countless beds filled with aged men, who apparently were in various stages of dying. As I started down a long, narrow aisle in my search for Tom, it seemed as though every old fellow who could muster the strength was propped up on his elbow and staring at me through pale watery eyes. I felt uncomfortable and asked one of them if he could direct me to Tom Sharkey. He smiled wanly and pointed a bony finger toward a far window and suddenly I spotted a shrunken man with thin gray hair rimming his bald head. He was almost completely enveloped in a faded green mandarin robe. I introduced myself as having grown up in Cripple Creek. I also brought him greetings from Lowell Thomas, who had once been a pupil of mine in the Victor High School.

When I complimented him on his elegant robe, he grinned happily and pulled himself higher on the pillows so that I could get a better view, not only of the robe but of the elaborately gold-embroidered sash that held it in place. His pride in this memento of his days of fighting glory was apparent in the nostalgic warmth of his eyes, as he smoothed a satin sleeve. "It was a present from my shipmates when I landed in America from Ireland in 1895. Wore it in the ring," he bragged, "with 'Big Jim' Jeffries—Bob Fitzsimmons —Joe Choynski—'Gentleman Jim' Corbett—" He chewed his gums reminiscently and smiled. "Guess the names of them boys don't mean a damn thing to you—you musta been just a kid then. My God!" he suddenly blurted out, "think of a nice girl like you growin' up in that hellhole of Cripple Creek! I hope you never was as miserable as I was. I had nothin' but trouble there—still have nightmares when I dream about what those sons of bitches done to me!"

"How did you happen to go there in the first place?" I asked, trying to divert him.

"I thought I'd strike a bonanza in the prize ring," he said, "but things didn't turn out that way. I arrived there from Denver," he went on, "in 1901, with some pugs named 'Spider Kelly,' Bob Armstrong, an' the 'nigger' Jack Johnson. Fightin' had been pretty slow down in the big city and I got the idea of throwin' exhibition matches for the minin' camps in Colorado an' Nevada, with us four fighters sparrin' each other an' offerin' to take on all comers. We started in Cripple Creek at the Grand Opera House. The first night was a sellout an' it looked hunky-dory for the outfit. But the second, third, and fourth nights, nobody showed up. We had no money, no backers, and no nothin', ab-so-goddamned-lutely nothin' was comin' in. Things began to look serious for me and my boxin' stars—we were on the rocks!

"We ran head over heels in debt," he continued, "an' had to move out of our plush quarters at the National Hotel. There wasn't enough boxin' fans in the District to keep us goin' for more than one match. Jack Johnson, the star of the group, had already knocked out 'Mexican Pete' Everett after twenty rounds, but now he had to turn cook in our rented shack. The debts continued to pile up. The butcher nagged us for money. When we couldn't pay, he gave us spoiled meat and chickens."

Tom suddenly sat up in his bed and began to laugh. "We had to take what we got," he went on, "and the butcher had to keep sendin' the better meat because we began to threaten 'im an' he was afraid of a bunch of heavyweights. Eventually two of the fellas pulled up stakes an' left camp, but Jack Johnson an' me, we stuck around for quite a while, waitin' for the breaks. Jack got a job as a roustabout in a saloon up in Poverty Gulch an' where he got enough to eat was anybody's guess. I fought everybody who come along no matter what was in the kitty. Nobody thought Jack would stop Tommy Burns, the World's Heavyweight champ in 1908, but hell, he coulda killed 'im if the police hadn't called a halt. Then, damned if he didn't go on to lick Jack O'Brien, Tony Ross, Stan Ketchel, and Jim Jeffries. He was working up to the big battle with Jess Willard."

Tom unfastened the green satin robe as if to breathe easier, and pushed it back from his chest, exposing a patch of curly gray hair. A nurse put another pillow under his shoulders and after a couple of deep sighs, he started to talk again. "This ticker of mine's no good," he said, smiling in apology. "Someday before long, it's goin' to run down, and the docs won't be able to wind it up again."

"What about Jack Johnson's fight with Jess Willard? If you feel up to it, please tell me," I said.

"I thought nobody had forgotten that," he said, giving me a reproving glance. "Willard knocked Jack out in twenty-six rounds down in Havana, Cuba, in 1915 and won the world's crown, but he held it only four years. A young up-start, named Jack Dempsey, soon settled his hash—punched 'im so hard that he failed to answer the bell in the fourth round. That was in December 1919—"

"Whatever happened to Jack Johnson?" I interrupted, having read something of his scandalous career.

"Kicked out of the U.S.A. in 1912 for violation of the Mann Act, and from then on, he fought in places like Australia, New Zealand, and Cuba. I heard that after his defeat by Willard he was givin' exhibitions in all the big cities in Europe—Paris, Berlin, Moscow, Budapest—but most fighters are soon forgotten, no matter how famous they was. Folks 're loyal to a champ while he lasts but usually fans 're fickle. They wash their hands of a guy when he starts to slip." A faraway look came into his eyes. "I read that Jack Johnson had been killed in an auto accident somewheres in Europe in 1946."

I saw that he was beginning to slump down in his bed and asked him if I could make him more comfortable. He smiled gratefully and leaned on my arm as I plumped up the pil-lows. "In my way of thinkin' Jack Johnson hadn't committed no worse sins than the rest of us in the game and a whole lot of others on the outside. We all lived rotten lives between bouts and the public overlooked it as long as we won the dough for 'em. He'd had more schoolin' than most fighters and a pretty good mother and father. He was crazy over his mother and talked about her a lot. I remember he called her Tiny. His old man was a caretaker of a schoolhouse in Galveston and on Sundays preached in a little church for the colored folks. But white people were prejudiced and jealous of Jack's victories in the ring and they set out to get him deported. He became a man without a country. The big thing against Jack Johnson was—he was black."

I didn't want to risk tiring him too much, but I began to realize that he had told me very little of his own stormy career in Cripple Creek. I pressed him further. "I understand you had some trouble in camp with 'Mexican Pete.'"

"I'd like to forget that," he said, flushing. "I'd never climbed into the ring with a yellower cur. It was the time us four fighters went to the District to put on exhibition matches. This Mexican challenged me and I agreed to go four rounds with him for a purse of twenty-five bucks. But the minute the bell rang in the first round, he grabbed me in a clinch. Hell, I couldn't make 'im uncover, an' if I did, back he'd come huggin' me like a polar bear! I was gettin' madder an' madder an' complained to the referee but got nowheres— for some reason, Pete was a favorite in camp; fans had bet a lot of money on 'im.

"Finally he came at me when the bell rang for the fourth, only to clinch again. I beat him to it this time an' with a right swing let 'im have it below the belt! The crowd went wild, yellin' foul an' cursin' an' hissin'. I forfeited the fight an' left town as fast as my legs could carry me. I'd heard that those folks in the Creek had been known to tar an' feather a pug they didn't like—"

He began to cough, his face turned paler, and his breathing was labored. He tried to reach for the medicine bottle on the table but was too weak to do more than point a finger and look at me with beseeching eyes. I glanced around anxiously for a nurse but none could be seen. I pressed a button to no avail. The label on the bottle read: "Nitroglyc-erin. To be taken as needed," and it dawned on me all at once that I had read it was the medication often given for sudden heart seizure. With a feeling of trepidation, I slipped a tablet under Tom's tongue and raised his head on the pillow. In a moment, to my intense relief, he began to breathe easier and smiled at me faintly as if to reassure me. "It's only this goddam ticker again," he said, regaining his voice. "Don't worry—I'm okay now. What was I tellin' you when—oh yes, about that bastard, 'Mexican Pete'—"

"Forget him, Tom" I said quickly, patting his hand. "Visiting hours are almost over and I must leave or a hospital orderly will throw me out. There's one thing more, though, I want to ask you, before I go. What do you remember as the highest peak of your life in and out of the ring?"

A broad grin spread over his wrinkled face. "It was the time I bet seventy-seven thousand dollars on Bob Fitzsimmons when he knocked out Jim Corbett in the championship fight in Carson City, Nevada, in 1897. But easy come, easy go. I was the top kingpin in boxin' for three or four years and then I landed in that goddamned Cripple Creek. I began to go downhill in the fightin' game from there on. Figgered I was gettin' too old an' threw in the sponge; and opened a saloon on Fourteenth Street in New York. It was a swell setup. Tim McGrath, my manager for years, suggested that all it needed was a huge chandelier in the center of the room. 'Hell,' I said, 'what's the use? I won't have nobody around who can play it!'

"After my wife died, I returned to Frisco, the best town on the map for pugilists. I thought maybe I could make a comeback. But I found out I was finished with the ring for good when my ticker began to act up, and it's been rough goin' for me ever since. But I like it here in Frisco. It's home. I've got lotsa friends—people drop by every day—"

He looked tired. I felt guilty and made excuses for having overstayed my time. He held up his knotted hand to wish me good-by. "I'd like to see a copy of that there book you're doin' about the Creek," he said. "Maybe you seen some gold in the dumps that I missed." He leaned back on his elbow just as the other men had done when I first arrived. "And let me ask a favor, please. Call up Jack McDonald again over at the *Call-Bulletin*. Tell 'im I want 'im to take you to Sartori's grill for dinner on me to celebrate the old days." He smiled and added, almost inaudibly, "God bless you and good-by, dear lady."

Tom Sharkey, born in Ireland in 1873, died in 1953, not long after my chat with him at the City and County Hospital. He was buried with military honors at the Golden Gate National Cemetery in San Francisco. His modest estate of a few hundred dollars was left to St. Patrick's Church for Masses for his wife, Katherine, and himself. The remainder, mostly donations from admirers, was turned over to the Columbia Park Boys Club to build a boxing room which was named for Sharkey. "He never wore the toga of a champion," Jack McDonald wrote in the *Call-Bulletin*, "but so long as there is prizefighting, his name will rank among the immortals of the ring."

And as a human being of stamina and grit, he will forever have an unforgettable place in my memory.

# IX

# The Manassa Mauler
# in Person

I found when I reached my daughter's home in North Hollywood that Lowell, with his customary dispatch, had sent word to her that he had talked with Jack Dempsey by telephone in Santa Monica and that I should call him as soon as possible to ask for an appointment. But on the very day of my arrival, a note came from the fighter himself, inviting me to have lunch with him on Friday, at Romanoff's, in Beverly Hills.

Romanoff's! I could hardly contain myself for excitement! My nearest approach to this famous restaurant had been in reading about it in Hedda Hopper's gossip column. It was one of the most exclusive gathering spots for celebrities in Southern California. Never in my wildest fantasies had I dreamed that someday I would be a guest there of the man

[117]

who was rated as the greatest fighter of all times. I accepted at once.

In spite of his fame, I felt at ease when we met in the softly lit foyer of Romanoff's dining room. His photographs, in and out of the arena down through the years, had been published so often in magazines and newspapers that it seemed as if I already knew him. There was no mistaking his tall, powerfully built figure, the thatch of dark hair and the high cheekbones suggestive of his Indian heritage. Also, I had spent most of the night before leaving Cripple Creek, pouring through his book, *Round by Round, An Autobiography,* which George Coplen had loaned me. I learned that he had been born the ninth of eleven children and the youngest of four boys, in Manassa, a tiny Mormon village of the San Luis Valley in Southern Colorado. He started life with the impressive name of William Harrison. The parents, Hiram and Celia, together with their eight siblings, had migrated from the mountain country of West Virginia where their forebears had picked up traces of Choctaw and Cherokee blood.

But the father was a kind of worthless fellow when it came to getting and keeping a job. Often the only money coming in was what he earned playing the fiddle, mostly "Turkey in the Straw" and "The Arkansas Traveller" at the church dances. But this was scarcely enough to feed the burgeoning family and pay the rent for the five-room house into which they were crowded. Celia, the strong, plucky mother, had to supplement their income by scrubbing floors, taking in washing, and mending clothes for her own as well as other people's children. She had great ambitions for her youngsters and often talked to them about the importance of getting an education so that the girls could marry good men and the boys would someday become rich and powerful gentlemen. Harry, as he was then called, and his younger sister, Elsie, were the only two who finished grammar school.

But the San Luis Valley offered marvelous playgrounds for an observing lad. It was surrounded by the Southern Rockies, where peaks often towered to an altitude of fourteen thousand feet and young rivers, like the Arkansas and Rio Grande, threaded courses through farmlands and cattle ranges to the Gulf of Mexico. The boy learned the ways of wild animals and how to hunt game for food as well as for sport. He became skillful at lassoing unbridled horses and broncobusting, and when there was nothing more exciting to do, the kids in town could always vent their spleen on each other and sometimes knock out a tooth or bloody a nose. "It was a great life for a punk like me," he said, when I mentioned having read the autobiography. "I can't remember when I didn't have a good time. As soon as my older brothers and sisters left home to strike out for themselves, I was sitting pretty, scrapping anybody that talked back to me."

But as I sat across from him, sipping a dry Martini at Romanoff's, it struck me all of a sudden that for some reason, this was not one of his happiest moments. He seemed awkward and embarrassed and stumbled over his words. I began to wonder what Lowell might have told him about me—that I had once been a school teacher, no doubt, or worse still, that I had been a college dean of women, a title that was chilling enough to frighten the most redoubtable prize fighter.

While I was pondering the situation, he leaned his head toward me and said in a low voice: "I hope you don't mind, but I've invited an old friend who's having lunch in the grill to bring his guest and join us later for dessert. I thought after I had given you the rough stuff on prizefighting, he might talk about what it's like to write prize-winning books. It'll be something on the cultural side. He's quite a famous author—you've probably read some of his stories. His name is

Gene Fowler and the Reverend with him is Father Rogers of Chicago who converted him to Catholicism, not so long ago. I told him that you had been a dean of women and that he must be on his best behavior."

This sudden windfall both amazed and amused me. Apparently Jack had arranged to count on Gene Fowler to save him in case he found himself in water too deep for him, with this friend of Lowell Thomas. "What an unexpected treat!" I said, genuinely delighted. "Of course, I am familiar with his Western books, especially those with a setting in Colorado. I only wish that I could take him aside and get a few pointers about how to write a best seller!"

Jack smiled in a pleased way and signaled the waiter. "Perhaps the lady would like another Martini," he said, and then looked questioningly at me. "How about it?" I hastened to say that two were my limit. "That's my limit too," he said, with a deceptive grin, and the waiter removed our glasses.

"Tell me, Jack"—already I had begun to call him by his familiar name as a fighter—"when did you first get the idea of becoming a professional boxer?"

"Damned if I know exactly. Maybe it was when my mother was running a boarding house in a mining camp, called Creede, about eighty-five miles from Manassa. I was around six years old and when I saw her hands bleed from scouring all those heavy pots and kettles and heard her groan with backache, getting down on her knees to scrub the floors, I used to tell her that someday I'd be a big man with lots of money and would buy her a fine house where somebody else would do all the hard work. But it was Bernie, my oldest brother, that I idolized, who gave me a hunch as to how I might make my stake for her come true.

"One summer, over in Creede," he went on, "Bernie was matched against a well-known local middleweight of that day, and knocked him out cold. From then on, he began to show me some of the tricks of the game, how to stand and snap away, how to make a fist, and side-step, and deliver a jab. By the time I was fifteen, I was a pretty good puncher. What really decided me, I guess, was the bout when Jack Johnson, the Negro, knocked out 'Big Jim' Jeffries, for the world's crown, in 1910, at Reno. I kept saying to myself from then on that Jack Johnson was the pug I'd have to beat someday." The waiter poured us some hot coffee and Jack went on with his story. "I began practicing in earnest to train myself for a boxing career, sparring with my brothers, punching bags, breathing deep, dodging, and practicing footwork. I massaged my arms and twisted broom handles with Johnny, my next older brother, and chewed resin to strengthen my jaw muscles, and I never walked when I went down the street—I always skipped rope."

"I wish you'd clear up something for me, Jack. It was said in Cripple Creek that you fought George Coplen so viciously because you were both romancing Georgia-Belle, the beautiful madam at the Mikado down on Myers Avenue. Was this so?"

He threw back his head and his huge frame shook with laughter. "I've heard that crazy yarn so often that if I didn't know it was a press agent's spout, I might come to believe it myself. Nope, honey"—we were on the honey basis now— "take it from me, it's plain hogwash. Coplen was a tough gutty fighter—who almost did me in and finished my career."

"I was also told in camp that you had been making quite a reputation for yourself, under the name of Jack Dempsey, boxing over in Utah, before your bout with Coplen."

"That's right. I copied the name from my brother Bernie, who inherited it from the well-known pugilist 'Jack Dempsey, the Nonpareil.'" He laughed at the recollection. "Then my brother Johnny got into the fight game and he too latched on to the moniker of 'Jack.' Seemed like it had become a family trademark. All of us boys grew up in the boxing game. Bernie, the oldest, was the best of the lot but he had a fairly short career. Went to work in the Golden Cycle on Battle Mountain and finally died of miners' consumption.

"It was Bernie that got me into that Coplen hassle. Fighting was in his blood and when he was challenged by the big guy, George Coplen, the camp's white hope for the World's Heavyweight Crown, he signed up for a purse of fifty bucks. But when he got a second look at Coplen's powerful build, he had a hunch that he'd made a mistake." He shook a cigarette from his monogrammed leather case and tapped it slowly on the back of his hand as if pondering the memory.

"That was in the late fall of 1914 or early '15," he went on, "and I was doing so well with my fists over in Provo that Bernie sent for me to come to the Creek. He said he had a good proposition to make me. When I arrived, he told me about his upcoming bout with Coplen. 'The truth is,' Bernie said, 'I don't feel up to it. I'm pushing forty and my health's bad. I want you to pinch-hit for me in that Coplen bout.' I hedged, wondering what the crowd would think of that last-minute switch, but Bernie claimed the fans wouldn't know the difference. 'Jack Dempsey would still be in there fighting, but their eyes, as well as their money, would be fixed on their Golden Boy, George Coplen!'

"That was one of the wildest guesses Bernie ever made," Jack snorted. "The mob caught on to me the minute I slipped through the ropes, and they were plenty mad! They cursed and booed and yelled, 'Throw 'im out!' I could almost see the rafters shaking in that old Lyric Opera House, and I was plenty scared, I can tell you, and wanted to turn tail and run, but there was Bernie, my second—he never took his eye off me. I was mad as hell at him for putting me up against that giant. I guess it got my dander up—the blood rushed to my head all of a sudden and I sailed into

[122]

George, at the bell, with a killer left, and down he went in a fast sprawl.

"I toppled him several more times in the first round, but he had the spring of a trampoline artist and always bounced up and came after me like a wild bull. He seemed to be getting stronger and gaining confidence as though suddenly aware that he was the two to one favorite in the District. The fans cheered and guffawed as if they tasted victory for their hero. Round after round, he hit the mat and just as often he pulled himself up ready to attack again." Jack took a big swallow of coffee and lit another cigarette. "It was between the sixth and seventh," he said, "when I told Bernie that I was all in and couldn't last much longer. 'He's as near dead as you are,' Bernie said, at the sound of the bell. 'Get in there, you bum, an' rush 'im—rush 'im, I tell you!'

"Somehow, I floored him again and again and every time he would bounce up like a tennis ball. I was too weak to land a punishing blow and groggy from the altitude. My lungs seemed to be collapsing and my feet felt heavy, but I kept whaling away. All George had to do was drag himself up from that floor one more time and I'd fall down in his place. He was that close to winning the decision. It was only the referee that saved me by stopping the fight with a technical knockout."

Jack leaned back in his chair and smiled at me reflectively. "You know," he said at last, "I don't ever remember being so down and out as I was after that Coplen fight. I was head over heels in debt and was going to have to muck again in the mines. My God! How I hated that prospect! I was as discouraged as hell. Worst of all—I wasn't as good as I thought I was. Self-confidence had always been one of my greatest assets. That string of wins over in Utah had made me sure I was unbeatable. Now that belief in myself was

[123]

seriously shaken. My eighth fight it was—and the toughest I had ever known. I walked twenty-five miles over the mountains to Cañon City and hopped a freight train back to Utah, so disheartened that I was on the verge of quitting boxing forever."

"But you couldn't give up," I put in, "it was in the blood, as you said of Bernie. The world and its rewards lay ahead of you—"

"Let's face it—I loved boxing. The crowd applauding and roaring approval thrilled me like nothing else I'd ever experienced. I wanted to give everything I had in the prize ring to deserve their enthusiasm as well as the money—the money I would need in gobs if I was ever going to build my mother the kind of home I dreamed of for her. In time, I cooled off from the Coplen fizzle, moved on from Utah to Nevada, and after three years of knocking around out West, lumberjacking, mining, sleeping in flophouses, I finally made enough from a couple of fights to go to New York."

"But that wasn't your Shangri-La either, was it?"

He nodded. "I found out it's true what they say about New York—you shouldn't go there until they send for you. After a string of matches with second-raters, I finally got two fights with Billy Miske, one of the best in the business, and through him I met Fred Fulton, the top challenger for Willard's world title. I trained hard for that fight with Fulton and my guarantee was for twelve thousand five hundred dollars, half of which was to go to my manager, Jack Kearns. That still left me enough dough for the five-thousand-dollar home in Bingham Canyon, Utah, I had in view for my mother. But the money didn't come through as I expected. It wasn't until I knocked out 'Cowboy' Jess Willard for the World's Heavyweight title in 1919, at Toledo, that I was able to get some cash ahead. After that, things looked up for me fast. Soon I was able to put a hundred thousand in a trust fund for my mother. Two years later I defeated Georges Carpentier, the Frenchman, to the tune of my first of three million-dollar gates."

"By that time," I said laughing, "you must have been able to buy one of those fabulous Mormon palaces for your mother in Salt Lake City!"

"I sure would've if one had been for sale. As it was, I found her a real nice place up on the hill where she could get a beautiful view of the city and the green valley beyond. I filled it with lots of expensive furniture and servants to do all the work. But she wasn't happy—said she was lonesome and didn't need servants to do the housework. So I bought another home for her in a fashionable neighborhood on East South Temple Street but she liked it even less. She couldn't think of anything to do to pass the time.

"Finally, a bright idea struck me. My own personal life hadn't been going too well. The money was rolling in but that wasn't what I needed. I had been married in 1933 to my third wife, Hannah Williams, a cute singer and dancer on Broadway. We pulled out for Hollywood where I was getting into movies and in the course of time, two little daughters, Barbara and Joan, were born. But Hannah was not the maternal type. She longed to return to the white lights and applause of New York. Pretty soon, I faced another divorce and was given custody of the two children. I didn't know what to do with them. I had to travel a lot and couldn't see them very often. So I bought a nice home in Santa Monica and hired a housekeeper and a governess and I'd hurry back between matches or movie locations and issue orders about how I wanted my girls brought up. But it was no go—it didn't work. The kids were getting out of hand. They needed to feel loved and guided by somebody who belonged to them. Then, it occurred to me that my own wonderful mother, who was pining away for someone to take care of over in

Salt Lake City, might be just what the doctor ordered for my youngsters. The reason I'd never thought of it before was that I felt she'd served her stretch after raising her own house full of children. I telephoned her and she must have fired the servants at once, locked up the mansion, and taken the next train to Los Angeles. It turned out fine," he concluded. "She and the girls have always been devoted to each other."

"They must be in their late teens, by now," I said, "and thinking about going to college."

He straightened his broad shoulders and his eyes filled with pride. "That's what they are aiming for—seems to me I stumble over catalogs every time I come back from a trip!"

Two men, one a priest, were coming toward our table. Jack saw them, smiled, and beckoned. "That's Gene now," he said, "and Reverend Rogers. I was beginning to think Gene had forgotten us. He's a busy fellow—understand he's working on a new book, himself—"

I recognized him from the pictures which always headed his feature stories in the Denver *Post*. He appeared to be in his mid-sixties. Age was thinning his gray hair and wrinkles had begun to etch the corners of his eyes. Colorado had proudly proclaimed him as a "Denver boy," after he went to New York in his early thirties to become sports editor of the *Daily Mirror,* and later stepped up to be managing editor of the *Morning Telegram.* I had not heard much of him, however, until he returned West and began to write such widely read books as *Timberline, Schnozzola,* and *Good Night, Sweet Prince,* the moving biography of John Barrymore.

He evidently noticed that Jack and I had finished dessert and were starting on a fresh round of coffee. "I looked in on you a little while ago," he said, after the introductions were over, "but Jack was holding forth so intently that I didn't have the heart to interrupt. I figured that he was probably telling you about that time back in twenty-three when Luis Firpo knocked him through the ropes and he landed in the press section—and almost lost his World's title."

"No," Jack said, with a wink, "I was giving her the low-down on 'the long count' when Gene Tunney put me out of the heavyweight race, in our second match in twenty-seven, out in Chicago. I shoulda won that decision but I was no strategist like Tunney—"

"Actually," I said, "he was telling me about his mother and his lovely daughters, and the home they had all made together."

"I understand you are going to write a book about the gold-rush years in Cripple Creek," he said, turning to me. "I used to go there as a cub on the *Post,* whenever a big match was scheduled, and I came to know a remarkable character named Otto Floto. He was much older than either one of us—maybe you've come across him in your reading. Every kid in the state knew Otto Floto, not as a colorful fight promoter, but for the 'Dog and Pony Show' and 'Sells-Floto Circus' which he took on tour every spring."

"I was not too young to remember going to those carnivals," I said, "and drinking pink lemonade, and riding the wooden ponies on the merry-go-round outside the big circus tent."

"He was the most enterprising fellow I ever knew," Gene went on. "There wasn't anything he couldn't do to make an honest buck. Dempsey, here, must have cut his eyeteeth on stories about Otto Floto. He was a natural fight promoter and for a time was manager for Bob Fitzsimmons.

"Wasn't he the guy, way back, who used to rake the saloons on Bennett Avenue for fighting drunks and make them punch it out for a dollar admission on the stage at the Butte Opera House?" Jack put in. "My God, what a man!" Even Father Rogers had to laugh at this sudden burst of irreverence. "Whatever became of him?" Jack asked, sweetening his coffee with several lumps of sugar. "He must have become one of those Cripple Creek Midases we see in the movies or read about in the papers!"

"He tried writing plays and didn't do badly," Gene continued, "but his heart wasn't in that sort of thing. He wanted showier, more exciting stuff, like putting on fights. The next thing I heard was that he had got a job as a sports reporter for the Denver *Post*. That's when he and I became close friends. He taught me newspapering from the ground up. I moved on to New York, finally, and he was promoted to be sports editor of his newspaper, a job that brought him nation-wide fame, and lent distinction to the sports pages of the Denver *Post*."

"What a thrilling story!" I said. "I hope you're planning to write Otto Floto's biography, someday, when you finish with the Hollywood scene."

"I have it vaguely in the back of my mind," Gene said, reaching for his rumpled pack of cigarettes, "but I don't know when I'll get around to it. When he died, he left me his book of clippings. It is a valuable bit of ring history." He looked at me thoughtfully for a moment. "Maybe it is something you'd like to read. I'll be glad to loan it to you, if you wish—"

I accepted the offer gratefully, but a quick reading made it clear to me that only an author of Gene Fowler's caliber could ever do justice to the life of Otto Floto.

The two hours with Jack Dempsey and the brief encounter with Gene Fowler passed too quickly. As we strolled slowly out to the foyer I said good-by to Gene and Father Rogers and stood talking for a few moments with Jack. "I have one or two more questions to ask you, before I go," I said. "How do you account for your great success? You must have a secret formula. You've won victory after victory in the ring, from knocking out Jess Willard to your own final defeat by

Gene Tunney. You were the first to fight to a million-dollar gate, you own 'Dempsey's' on Broadway, every bit as famous as Romanoff's, you have property from New York to California, you're a board director of a technical training school for boys in Chicago. And best of all, you must have, literally, thousands of friends, all over the world. Are there any magic rules or words to go by?"

"Don't get the idea, honey, that it's all been easy," he said, touching my shoulder as if for emphasis, "I've known the depths and I've worked hard to pull myself up. But I've been lucky, too," he added, smiling. "I've also had a motto to live by. I'll share it with you. It'll work for anybody who's not determined to stay flat on his back. Sit tall, stand tall, walk tall, and think tall—nothing is so important as thinking tall."

"There's one other favor I'd like to ask," I said, with an apologetic feeling of shyness. "Please, Jack, would you write your autograph in my little black book?"

"Sure, honey." He laughed, reaching for his pen and scribbling his name hurriedly. "Now you're eligible for membership in the Jack Dempsey fan club!"

He walked with me outside and spoke to the doorman about calling a cab for me. But I declined, saying I would rather walk, since I had one or two errands to do in Beverly Hills. We shook hands again and he said: "Let me know the next time you come to New York. I'll arrange a luncheon at 'Dempsey's' and invite Lowell Thomas, Gene Tunney, and another great guy, Eddie Eagan. Don't forget—it's a date!"

# X

# The Kansas Tornado
# Strikes Camp

So much had happened during my five or six days in
California that it seemed decades since I had last seen
Bennett Avenue. It was like coming home to be welcomed
by the Ragles at the Old Homestead, to gossip with Mrs.
Oliver again at the Court House and pass along Jack Demp-
sey's greetings to George Coplen. It was good to have dinner
at the Imperial with Grace Eads and to laugh over Tom
Sharkey's refusal to put a chandelier in his New York saloon
because he didn't have anyone to play it. Grace remembered
Tom well and how he skipped camp when the fans
threatened to tar and feather him after he fouled "Mexican
Pete."

But a sense of guilt began to haunt me. The weeks were
flying by and I still hadn't visited with all the interesting
old-timers or finished reading the newspapers stored at the

mill. In order to refresh my memory, I reviewed the copious notes which I had culled from the old issues of the *Morning Times*. Some of the events had been underscored as being especially dramatic, amusing, or flavorful. Once I came upon a story that I, myself, vaguely recalled. It happened over in Cripple Creek, during my first year of teaching in the Victor High School.

One morning, a dispatch appeared in the *Times* that sent cold shivers through the District's underworld. Everybody was talking about it. The shock couldn't have been worse if Big Bill Heywood had suddenly come marching around Gold Hill leading a battalion of the Western Federation of Miners. The famous camp had suffered many catastrophes during its years of activity, deadly epidemics, mass murders, blizzards, bloody strikes, but nothing ever packed the potential horror of that news item. Carry Nation, the "Kansas Tornado," it read, was heading, armed with hatchet and hymnbook, for the Cripple Creek District and had threatened to smash every beer joint and dive from Poverty Gulch to Squaw Mountain.

People in camp had been joking and wisecracking about Carry's saloon-gutting antics ever since she began in 1901 to clean out Wichita's bootlegging gin mills. Kansas, a Prohibition state, had been notoriously wet for more than twenty years and Carry declared that she had been "called of God" to destroy the evil. At first, she went armed with only a hand organ and planted herself in front of illicit speak-easys, singing "Nearer, My God, to Thee." When crowds gathered around to jeer and heckle, she decided on more belligerent tactics. Substituting an iron rod and later a hatchet for the hand organ, she marched boldly into the "dens of rum and wickedness" and shattered bars, glasses, bottles—everything breakable in sight.

"Saloon habitués in Cripple Creek," the *Times* went on

to say, "have roared with laughter at Carry's command of profanity. She could have taught Jack Johnson and Peg Leg
McGinty a word or two. Police in Wichita had to cower
or avoid her flailing hatchet when they tried to arrest her.
'Get out of my way,' she yelled. 'Keep your dirty hands off
me, you rum-soaked, whisky-swilled, saturnine-faced sots!'
When finally summoned before the judge, she addressed him
as 'Your Dishonor' and then held her nose and gagged. 'Let
me outta here before I puke,' she ordered. 'Government is
like rotten fish—it always stinks worse at the head.' "

I, a proper school teacher across the mountains in Victor,
had heard only repercussions of the fracas. I wondered in
reading about it almost fifty years later if anyone was left
in camp who could give me a blow-by-blow account of
Carry's singlehanded war on vice in Cripple Creek. Then,
one afternoon, I happened to meet Ben Hill coming out of
the post office and we walked up Bennett Avenue together.
Ben, a native of Texas, was known as a great storyteller.
He was a pioneer from way back and one of the few
graduate mining engineers in camp. His hair was gray, now,
but he was still slender and good-looking. I remembered that
he was once considered quite a catch among the older girls of
the Klover Klub crowd. He was known especially for his
droll humor and keen memory of past events.

We walked slowly up the street recalling old times, at
random, the friends who had moved away or died, the
colorful parades that enlivened the town, the terrifying catastrophes, the fantastic men and women who sometimes
raised hell in camp and were sent away for a spell at the
State Penitentiary in Cañon City, or to the "crazy house"
down in Pueblo.

It was five o'clock when we reached Third and we stood
for a few moments watching the tourists pour down the hill
from the matinee in the theater in the Imperial's basement.

Some climbed noisily into their big cars and sped away. But most began strolling along the Avenue as if looking for something more to do to kill time until François, the famed chef at the hotel, would offer his own flavorsome concoctions for their enjoyment. Unlike the early years, there was little to see, no titillative places to go, such as Tom Lorimer's saloon with its ladies' entrance, or the Butte Thirst Parlor with its phonograph records banging out all the latest hits, or Jim Hanley's Pool and Billiard Hall, or Johnny Nolon's elegant gambling emporium across on the corner.

"I never look at those boarded-up windows over there at Nolon's," Ben said, "without getting a kind of twinge in my heart. There wasn't a nicer fellow in the District than Johnny Nolon and he ran a strictly first-class saloon and gambling outfit." Ben went on nostalgically, "Never stood for drunks on the premises nor crookedness at faro or blackjack. If a man got down on his luck, Johnny was the first to help him up on his feet again. But he was never the same after what Carry Nation did to his place—"

"I've been wanting to hear that story," I interrupted. "I was teaching school over in Victor at the time and only caught snatches of the affair the next day. Tell me all about it sometime."

He glanced at his watch suddenly and his eyes brightened. "Why don't you come on up to our house now?" he said, taking my arm. "The missus will fix us a cup of tea, or something with more authority if you prefer, and we can have a good visit. I have an interesting scrapbook of clippings about some of the big events in camp—maybe you'd like to see it. I wasn't married at the time and later when my wife was cleaning out the drawers, she came across the scrapbook and all the clippings about Carry Nation's smashing up Cripple Creek. She gets a great kick out of reading them

[133]

from time to time. I'll tell her to look for the book some-place and we can go through it."

I did not need any urging. I had met Norma Hill several times and been entertained in their home. She had been a Texas belle and apparently nothing delighted her more than having company and relating some of her own tenderfoot experiences in the rip-roaring mining camp of the early 1900s. She seemed very pleased to see me and had no trouble finding Ben's well-worn collection of clippings.

"Actually," Ben said, as he brought out a bottle of bourbon, "nobody ever took the threat of Carry's visit very seriously, even when they saw her striding down the steps at the Midland Terminal Depot. A crowd gathered around as soon as word spread of her presence. She was a husky woman, built more like a man, with her square determined jaw and muscular hands. She had no difficulty in elbowing her way to the sidewalk. Only the Salvation Army, evidently, knew that she was about to descend on Cripple Creek and the members welcomed her with drum and bugle and sang 'Onward Christian Soldiers.'"

Norma handed me the album of clippings. "Some of these stories," she said, "are from the *Morning Times,* others came from the Colorado Springs *Gazette* and the Denver papers sent to Ben by friends. Maybe you would like to read a few of them aloud," she went on. "They always give me a laugh."

The first one I picked up was from the *Morning Times,* which I had read before but had forgotten. It told of Carry's arrival in camp:

> Although she is six feet tall and not quite sixty, she appeared dumpy and old as she stepped down from the train and began to search for her baggage. One of the Salvation Army men started to help her, but she shoved him away. "Here you!" she shouted to a nearby express-man, "take my bags up to the Collins Hotel and say I'll

be there shortly." Then, all of sudden she stiffened; a limp cigarette was hanging from the fellow's lips. "Throw that stinkin' weed away!" she commanded, and her deep-set eyes snapped under their bushy brows. "But, lady," he protested in a mollifying tone, "it ain't lighted—" "Makes no difference," she replied heatedly. "Take it outta your trap or I'll do it for you and smack you in the bargain." He let the forlorn fag fall to the platform and a mob of small boys pounced on it before it rolled down the steps.

"It didn't take long before news of Carry's arrival swept through the camp and created panic in the dives on Myers Avenue," Ben put in, "and the hundred or so saloons on Bennett. Owners began to batten down their valuable plate-glass windows and locked their doors. Some hid the varicolored bottles reflecting their contents so temptingly in the bar mirrors. Others just steeled themselves and waited with one eye on a quick getaway through the alley.

"Johnny Nolon took a different tack. He told everybody that he wasn't goin' to let any woman, even Carry Nation, buffalo him. 'Let 'er come into my place, if she wants,' he said, 'and preach to the fellas. Haven't I always been on good terms with the lads in the Salvation Army? And don't I let the lassies step inside on cold winter nights and pass their tambourines among the boys who fill 'em up with gold pieces. And didn't I serve the whole band hot coffee and pretzels the time of the big blizzard? Let 'em come,' he went on cockily, 'and welcome to Carry and all the thirsty customers who pack in after her.'

"A huge crowd of onlookers and miners off shift over-flowed the sidewalks and street, as she started down from the depot," Ben continued. "No one seemed to believe for a moment that Carry could be stopped by a few bolted doors and boarded-up windows. Some fellows even hoped

[135]

to see a few stray bottles of Kentucky bourbon flying through the air. The mob around Johnny Nolon's was tense and restive. Already she had passed the National Hotel Bar only a block away. The thump of the Salvation Army drums was growing closer. A large poster displayed by an attractive young lassie invited one and all to attend Carry's lecture that night at Army Hall, when she would tell her intimate life story. 'Come and be saved from Demon Rum' the poster pleaded, 'before the light fails!'"

"Here's something from the *Morning Times* that's rather funny," Norma interrupted, pointing to a clipping and reading it aloud:

> Instead of entering Nolon's saloon, as everybody predicted, the little procession crossed over and continued down Third Street to Myers Avenue, "the wickedest two blocks this side of Sheol." By now it was joined by throngs of yelling little boys, on foot and riding donkeys, begging for toy hatchets which Carry was known to keep in her portmanteau to sell at twenty-five cents apiece. Dogfights and runaway teams added to the general commotion. But oddly enough, no "fallen women" were in sight. It was four o'clock in the afternoon, the hour when the crib inmates usually bestirred themselves and came outside in bright wrappers to gossip and smoke cigarettes with their neighbors.
>
> But today the blinds were drawn tight at the wedge-shaped windows; not a cough could be heard; not a thread of smoke floated from the spindly stovepipes. A nondescript cat streaked in front of the paraders and was chased up a telephone pole by a yellow mongrel. Except for the crusaders and camp hangers-on, Myers Avenue was as dead as a doornail. Not a brothel was open for Carry to "clean up"; not a single hesitant customer was left to be turned into paths of righteousness. It was hard to tell from the set expression on Carry's face whether

she was pleased or disappointed. "These harlots can't play possum with me," she called out for all to hear. "I'll come back tonight after my lecture and give them a raiding that'll knock 'em outta business for keeps!"

Norma sat back in her chair, smiling, when she had finished.

"Did you go to her lecture that night?" I asked Ben.

"I wouldn't have missed it for anything," he said. "Good Lord, outside of prize fights, the biggest amusements in camp were the old-fashioned gospel revivals. Capacity audiences filled their tents with shouting, singing, and confessions of sin. At the close, when guilty folks were entreated to come forward and throw themselves on God's mercy, the first to hit the sawdust trail were the old topers, whose good resolutions stretched only as far as the Branch Saloon or Crapper Jack's dance hall."

We all had a good laugh for a few moments and Ben fixed himself another drink. "This night was no exception," he put in. "'They were all there, sitting on the window sills, propped against the walls, waiting for Carry to stop long enough in her harangue against vice and liquor to give them a chance to take the pledge and witness for the Lord."

"Here's another funny one," Norma said, putting the album on her lap and turning a page. "Someone sent it to Ben from the Colorado Springs *Gazette*," and she read it to us:

Before plunging into her story at Army Hall she spoke appreciatively of the enthusiastic reception which Cripple Creekers had given her. "I knew I was needed here," she said, "for this foul cesspool is the most lawless and wicked spot in the country. Its red-light district and saloons, its gambling tables and wide-open houses of shame, places like the Old Homestead, have lured hundreds of men and women to death and destruction.

There was a scraping of feet and coughing as if people were uncomfortable. Then she went on to say that she had been agreeably surprised to see that many of Bennett Avenue's grogshops had already gone out of business. Johnny Nolon's was the one exception, and he had sent word, inviting her to come down there after the lecture and preach to the boys around the bar and tables. "That's the first time," she added sardonically, "that any liquor dealer ever laid himself wide open for a smashing!"

She waited a moment for the snickering to die down, but there was no smiling from the grim-faced women. They sat straining for every word, hope burning in their eyes. "My heart goes out to you in pity," she began, addressing them direct. "Like many of you, I was once alone and suffering and didn't know where to find help. At last God revealed that I, myself, should take matters in hand, that I should destroy all saloons and houses of ill-fame along with the swine that fatten on them."

"I recall that she had been married twice," Ben put in, "first to a brilliant doctor, but a slave to cigarettes and whisky—she was bitter against all fraternal orders, like the Masons, because they permitted members to stock their lockers with liquor. Poor woman," he said, "I can see her there telling how much she loved her husband and wanted only to make a home for him and their expected baby, but he had only one master, whisky. She told about looking through the streets for him night after night," Ben continued, "peering into saloons, trying to find him, but he guzzled his liquor at the Masonic Lodge where no woman was allowed to enter."

He picked up the album and fingered through the pages before handing it to me. "Here's one you should read," he said, "it's from the Denver *Post* and very sensational.

[138]

Women's sobs could be heard all over the big room, and men cleared their throats and blew their noses. "What could I do?" she continued hoarsely. "I was six months pregnant and my prayers had been of no avail. I beseeched the Masons to rescue my husband, to tear out the locker where he kept gin and whisky. But they called me a nuisance and ordered me to stay away from the lodge hall. Even church people turned deaf ears to my pleas and the ministers laughed when I begged them to direct the might of the Lord against blind pigs and fraternal orders." Her voice lowered and seemed on the point of breaking. "I spent agonizing hours on my knees, praying that my man would sober up and be a good husband. But he only went from bad to worse. He lost his patients and my friends avoided him. The baby was due and there was no money for food or medicine. Out of my desperation grew a bitter hatred, a loathing of saloons, prostitution, and tobacco which debauch and destroy the lives of innocent women and children. The world had become a place of misery for me," she said, her whole body trembling with emotion, "and it was then and there that a vision came to me and I heard God's command to fight unto death this inhumanity to mankind." Then she added quietly, "Six months later my beloved husband died of acute alcoholism."

"When she finished her sermon, there was an uneasy stirring in Army Hall," Ben put in. "Fellows who had been standing were starting to leave. 'Slim' Hardy, one of the camp's familiar drunks and a regular confessor at gospel meetings, lumbered down the aisle and held up his hand to take the pledge. 'God bless you, brother,' Carry screamed, 'let's all join in singing 'Blest Be the Tie That Binds.'"

"That's not all," Norma said, "read the rest of it, Ben." But Ben was apparently tired and gave the book to her and she continued where he had left off.

In spite of all the suffering her husband had caused her, his death had left her lonely and forlorn. She longed only for a kind, loving mate who would be a good father to her baby, now a year old. "A few months after the doctor's death I married David Nation," she went on, "but from the beginning he was cool toward me, completely lacking in affection, and worse still, indifferent to my little girl. He claimed that she was mentally defective and didn't want her on his hands. In time I, too, realized that the child wasn't normal and the old hatred of liquor began again to eat into my vitals"—her tone became hard and brittle—"and it was borne in on me that her father's besotted drunkenness had destroyed my baby's brain. It was then I swore to God that I would smash every low-down whisky joint in the state of Kansas!"

But apparently David Nation was a finicky fellow—he didn't like to see his wife's name splashed across the front pages of newspapers as a saloon smasher. He accused her, she said, of being as much of an outlaw as the bootleggers she despised. He was ashamed of her for wanting to make the state a better place for decent folks to live in, and before long he divorced her. She swore that as the Almighty was her witness, nothing would stand between her now and her oath to God to wipe from the face of the earth the scourges of booze, tobacco, and harlotry!

Johnny Nolon's place occupied the choicest corner on Bennett Avenue and was by all counts the plushiest saloon and gambling emporium in the District. Its red velvet draperies and thick carpets gave it the atmosphere of dignity and seclusion. Loose, raucous laughter never broke through the gilded screens behind the swinging doors; inebriated patrons were always eased out by way of the alley. It was understood that Johnny, "a gambler's gambler," expected his customers to behave like gentlemen while under his roof; he boasted of his exclusive trade. Faces of the District's leading million-aires and promoters were often reflected in the long, polished mahogany bar and the beveled glass mirror on the wall be-hind. A crystal chandelier, one of the few in camp, danced and sparkled in the breeze from the open transoms. But the pride of Johnny's life was the full-size painting above the mirror of "Venus Emerging from the Sea," seductively naked and buoyed by a shoal of frolicking dolphins. Some-times when the rooms were aired in the morning, the screens were pushed aside and the doors propped open so that children on their way to school could catch glimpses of Johnny Nolon's masterpiece.

"After the meeting in Army Hall," Ben went on, fixing himself another drink, "I strolled down to Johnny Nolon's to see if there was any excitement. Bennett Avenue in front of the saloon was packed with an eager throng of spectators, heckling Carry Nation, as she barged into Johnny's saloon, flanked by the Salvation Army. I moved in closer where I heard everything and saw what was going on. Johnny greeted Carry affably, showed her around briefly, and then invited her to say a few words of inspiration to the boys. Her face was stolid; the battle cry was in her voice. 'Marching as to—'

"Suddenly she stopped as if struck by a thunderbolt. She stood transfixed, staring wildly at Venus innocently emerging from the ocean. 'Hang some blankets on that trol-lop at once!' she screamed. Confusion reigned; there were no blankets in Nolon's place. Carry started to yank at one of the red velvet draperies, but someone pulled her away. 'Take your hands off me!' she shrieked. 'If that naked wench ain't covered up instanter, I'll cut her to shreds!' And with that she pulled her hatchet from beneath her duster, ran behind the bar, and started slashing first the mirror and then the painting above it. Johnny shouted at her in vain. He pleaded with the Salvation Army members to halt the woman. But their mission was peace, not brawls, and when they saw what was happening, they vanished as if by magic. The other onlookers seemed paralyzed by the ferocity of the attack, that is, until bottles of rare Scotch whisky began to roll from the shelves and spill on the carpet. The melee that resulted in the scramble to scoop it up was the worst Cripple Creek had seen since the wildest gold-rush years."

Norma showed me the final clipping in the album. It was one of those boxed items taken from the *Morning Times,* the day following Carry's foray with "Venus Emerging from the Sea." It read:

When Sheriff Henry von Phul arrived he had to pull Johnny from under a heap and put handcuffs on Carry before marching her off to jail. The whole camp was in an uproar, betting on what would happen next. The good women offered to take Carry into their homes for the night, but the men were all for "running her off the hill." The Salvation Army had no money to pay her fine of fifty dollars, and businessmen were afraid of bailing her out. It began to look as if she would have to sleep on the floor in the lockup. But Johnny Nolon, a true sport, although considerably bruised and patched, unexpectedly appeared before the judge and offered to pay the fine on condition that she'd take the midnight train for Denver. "I guess I had it coming to me," he said a bit apologetically. "It was one time I outsmarted myself. I'm bloody but unbowed," he added with a wry grin. "Johnny Nolon's will be open for business as usual tomorrow!"

Carry looked mighty pleased with herself, it was said, when the sheriff put her on the train. She promised to return in the near future and "clean out those dives on Myers Avenue." But her brief and stormy career was drawing to a close. Her last raid was in Butte, Montana, in 1910, and the public had lost its zest for Carry's saloon-smashing crusades. Without notoriety and headlines she herself grew less zealous in her goal to save the world from sin and destruction. She died in 1911 of what was termed "nervous exhaustion" but which doctors diagnosed as paresis.

# XI

# The Boilermaker

Sunset was fading by the time I started back down the road from my lively visit with the Ben Hills. Their two-story, bright yellow house with its white trim stood prominently on the corner of Eaton Avenue overlooking the Imperial, little more than a block below on Third Street. As I reached the hotel, a delicious whiff of something like curried lamb slowed my steps. I was pondering the temptation to indulge in one of François' celebrated dinners when I heard a woman's voice calling, "Hoo, hoo!" and I turned to see Agnes Dewar standing in the doorway at the Hoot Mon and beckoning as if she wanted to tell me something.

I hurried over and to my surprise she invited me in. Mrs. Oliver had told me that Agnes, in all her forty years in camp, had never mixed much with others and no one was ever seen calling on her except Millie Laveley, the saloonkeeper down on Myers Avenue, who died quite a while ago. "Folks seemed to think there was something queer," she said, "about her and Jack living together just as though they were man and wife, so they left them alone." I followed her through the dimly lit hall to their apartment at the back of the building. An enormous furnace dominated the combination living room and kitchen. A closed door at the left apparently led to the sleeping quarters.

"Sit down over there," she said, pointing to an ancient, overstuffed chair, "while I put some gasoline on a few chunks of coal to burn up the leftovers from supper and warm the place a bit. The walls of the furnace were completely lined with water pipes and in a few moments the radiator in the hall began to hiss and crackle. "It sure gets chilly up here in the Crik," she said, wiping her hands on a towel, "the minute the sun goes down!"

I asked about Jack, half-expecting him to emerge from a bedroom. But she said he wasn't home. "We have supper 'round four o'clock so's he can go to his souvenir stand in time to ketch the trade when the matinee's over." She went on to tell how he often stayed downtown after the night show. It seemed to me that her life must be grim and lonely most of the time and that she had called me over for company. While I was speculating about it, she suddenly asked if I were still living with the Ragles at the Old Homestead.

"Yes," I said. "I have been very comfortable there. My only complaint is that I have to eat out every day. I'd like to have a hot plate or a kitchenette so I could prepare my own meals—"

"You going to be in camp much longer?" she interrupted, rather cautiously.

"I'm not sure," I said. "I still have some reading to do in the old newspapers stored at the Carlton Mill; and there are several old-timers—your brother Jack is among them—with whom I want to talk about the early days. I should really leave in another month before snow begins to powder the mountains."

[145]

"Another month," she repeated, half to herself, and then her face brightened. "You remember asking me to let you know if we ever happened to have a vacancy?"

I nodded. "You weren't very encouraging then."

"Well, the man upstairs left. Got a better job over in Leadville. The apartment is for let. I'll show it to you now if you're still interested."

The thought of moving again so soon didn't appeal to me, but I was curious about the place. When I was a child, those upstairs rooms were the private offices of the Telephone Company where children never dared to venture. I reasoned, now, that no harm could come if I just looked around for old time's sake. Agnes switched on the shaded lamp that hung down from the skylight above a large, round dining table. The central lobby was furnished with a mirrored sideboard, several odd chairs, a couch, and a variety of outmoded accessories—crocheted doilies and tidies, hand-painted china vases filled with paper American Beauty roses, embroidered sofa pillows—treasures which Agnes had probably accumulated with the passing years. Everything was neat and clean. Not a speck of dust could be seen anywhere.

Two small rooms, a parlor and a bedroom, opened off the lobby. Their windows looked down dizzily on the steep cement sidewalk of Third Street and across to the Imperial Hotel with its lights aglow. An old upright piano with a hymnal on top and a few pieces of sheet music in the rack stood against a wall of the parlor. A settee, Morris chair, and chenille-covered table completed the furnishings. As we started out, I noticed a closed door and tried the knob, thinking that it led to another room. But it was locked. Agnes said that it only went up to the attic where Jack stored his specimens for the souvenir stand. "He always keeps the key," she added in a low voice, "in his vest pocket."

At the alley or far side of the lobby were the bathroom

and a commodious kitchen. The first things I noticed were the refrigerator and gas range—just what I'd been wanting! I felt myself weakening further as Agnes opened the cupboard doors full of shiny pots and pans and some Worcester china dishes which she said she had brought all the way from Scotland, after her mother's death. I began to have a nice, homey feeling about the place. For a moment I saw myself settled at the Hoot Mon Apartments in Cripple Creek for the rest of my days, just like the other old-timers. I put my arm around Agnes' shoulders and blurted out impulsively, "I'll take it. How much is the rent?"

"Forty dollars a month—in advance," she said very crisply, as if suspecting me of warming up to her for a bargain. "You'll have to furnish your own blankets and sheets."

"But I haven't any bedding with me," I said, my heart sinking.

"You might try renting some at the Imperial," she suggested. "I've heard they do that sometimes when the season's slack—like in September."

Everything worked out fine. The hotel supplied me with all the clean bedding I needed. Bob Ragle went out of his way to take me back and forth to the Mill and Agnes melted a bit and brought me some scones whenever she made them for Jack. I felt oddly at home among the old-fashioned tidies and fancy sofa pillows. They reminded me of our house on Golden Avenue when I was a child long ago and the times my mother taught me how to crochet. I was nearing the end of my summer in the District and wanted to hold back the fleeting weeks.

I had started my browsing through the old issues of the 1896 newspapers published shortly after the great fires. I had followed the course of events, the coming of the rail-roads, the fabulous gold strikes, the labor troubles, the garish parades and funerals, the prize fights and theatrical shows, the murders, and ill-fated individuals who lost their souls as well as their bonanzas, until I had come to the years 1918 and 1919, the last volumes to be stored in the Mill's attic.

The end of World War I in November 1918 had brought tragic times to the Cripple Creek District. Many of its finest young men died on the battlefields of Europe, and there was no armistice with a plague called the Spanish Influenza. It had swept across the Atlantic Ocean and into the cities and towns of the East as fast as a man could travel. But Cripple Creekers were congenital optimists and never believed that the worst could happen to them until it struck with deadly aim. "No flu bug," Oscar Burnside said when a few people began to get a little nervous, "could ever last long in this altitude." Johnny Nolon, a gambler of the highest integrity, added his word of cheer. "Even if there was one or two cases of the disease in camp," he said, "our fine doctors could root it out, goddamn pronto. There's no need for anyone to get panicky."

Meanwhile, the people carried on their usual duties and preoccupations. News dispatches were mostly of local interest: plans were under way to junk the Midland Terminal Railroad—the Short Line, the only road left in camp, would run from Divide to Cripple Creek—the red-light houses on "Iniquity Row" over in Victor were to be torn down—the Fleur de Lis Club was going to give a bridge luncheon at the home of Mrs. Frank Large—Lowell Thomas had written his wife's mother in Denver that he was on his way to the Holy Land by airplane.

Then, almost overnight, it seemed, the news items began to flare into headlines. The influenza germs which had started in Spain were said to be air-borne from the contaminated battlefields of Europe. Suddenly, so the frightening news ran, there were three thousand cases reported in Quincy, Massachusetts, and thirty cases were found in Boulder, Colorado.

Army camps were especially hard hit. A new antiflu serum was being tested at Camp Devins.

But even yet Cripple Creekers were not too much concerned. They were busy selling Liberty Bonds and Saving Stamps. Small dinner parties, however, refrained from serving wheat bread and sugar. It was a jolt to the District to hear that a death due to the flu had occurred at Colorado College in Colorado Springs. An editorial in the Cripple Creek *Times* of October 3, 1918, read:

> What is this new disease? Is it another German offensive? We think the more plausible explanation is that it is sickness caused by the recent cold snap which caught the country unprepared, dwellings were unheated, people had inadequate clothing. This is the season of the year when colds are frequent and often result fatally. There is no occasion for special concern, alarm or panic. The American Medical profession is perfectly capable of handling the situation and measures will be taken to check and destroy this virulent bug.

But the flu germs apparently didn't read editorials; they continued to spread at a calamitous rate, striking down victims in Denver, Colorado Springs, and Pueblo. People seemed to lose their heads. In Salida, two Mexican railroad workers were painted yellow because they refused to buy Savings Stamps. Cripple Creek killed its dogs and cats by the dozen because of the rumor that they were carriers of the disease. Churches, schools, and theaters were closed, but, although it was Prohibition time, saloons were allowed to keep their back doors unlocked because of the "curative virtue" of whisky in fighting the plague. Mortuaries were full and overflowing with corpses, and there were not enough coffins to bury them. Funerals formed almost a steady procession to Pisgah Graveyard, and fires were kept burning at night to warm the weary sextons.

At last Teller County was quarantined. The Cripple Creek *Times* evidently ran out of editorial advice and inspiration and began to publish instead homemade remedies offered by its subscribers. Among them was the following "Pneumonia cure":

> Take 6–10 onions, according to size, chop fine and put in large skillet over a hot fire. Add a quantity of rye meal and vinegar—enough to form a thick paste. Mix well and put in a cotton bag large enough to cover the lungs and apply as hot as the patient can bear. In about ten minutes apply another and repeat until patient is out of danger.

This prescription led to a shortage of vinegar and rye meal at the grocery stores, but there was no record of it having saved any lives. Doctors published the usual rules about getting plenty of sleep, avoiding persons afflicted with colds and sore throats, and not expectorating in public. But the flu germs were no respecters of persons and the overworked physicians sickened and died along with their patients.

A feeling of anguish came over me as I read of the District's hour of travail and one day I decided to go home early on a passing truck. The driver let me off at the post office. The mail hadn't come in yet and I had a little time to kill. Leslie Wilkinson, the postmaster, asked me to sit down and wait in his office. He was a cordial, friendly man, much younger than most of the old-timers I knew. I told him that I had been reading about the influenza epidemic and the havoc it had wrought in Cripple Creek.

"Yes, it was terrible," he said. "I was only sixteen at the time and I guess our whole family would have been wiped out if it hadn't been for Dr. W. W. King and the 'Boiler-maker.'"

"Oh, I knew Dr. King when I was a girl here—a rather

short man of slender build and a long Roman nose—I think I'd know him anywhere even after fifty years."

"We've always had wonderful physicians in the District," he replied, "but no one was ever better loved than Dr. King. When the flu hit camp, he worked night and day, driving his horse, Black Bess, all over town and even to the little settlements in the hills outside. Once there were four hundred deaths up here in six weeks. The hospitals were full and there was a frightful shortage of nurses." Leslie turned in his swivel chair and began to make doodles on a memo pad. "Dr. King sent out an appeal for the wives and mothers in the District to volunteer, but they held back, fearful of catching the disease and carrying it to their own families. Then, one day as he walked along Bennett Avenue, wondering where next to turn for help, he met a well-known denizen of the row, named Heller—Mrs. George Heller. I don't know why but everybody in town knew her as the Boilermaker. She collared him and said she'd heard he was calling on folks to nurse the sick and she'd like to take a swing at it, said she's always had a knack for taking care of sick people."

Leslie suddenly broke into a laugh. "The Doc later said he didn't welcome the idea of taking her on, much as he needed help. One look at the Boilermaker was enough to kill anybody already on the verge of the grave! She was a six-footer, strong and husky, and about fifty years old, and could outlift the heftiest miner. She'd been known to give old man Heller, her husband, many a sound thrashing when he came home drunk. The Doc, as you remember, was a slight fellow and he evidently thought it better not to tangle with the Boilermaker. So, he sent her to a cabin up on Globe Hill to look after a fellow who was recovering from pneumonia. But darned if she didn't quit the next day, and go for the Doc with fire in her one good eye." Leslie continued, chuckling in recollection, "She swore that the man on Globe Hill was 'well enough to take care of hisself.' She wanted to go only where she could help folks get well and save their lives; and Dr. King told her to come to our house.

"One of my brothers had died in the epidemic. My mother, father, and two other children were critically sick. I was the only one around to take care of them. I can still see the Boilermaker that first night, when she was getting ready for bed on the sofa. I had to sit up in a rocking chair because there was no place for me to lie down in our little house. I had seen her before, a long time ago when I was four or five. She lived in a cabin then, not far from us, and I often ran away from home, especially when I smelled cookies baking. I'd sit on her doorstep and wait until she'd give me some when they were done, and then she'd take me by the hand back to my mother. After she and George moved out of the neighborhood I never saw much of her again.

"Now I was a boy in my middle teens, the flu had laid low the rest of my family and I was in desperate trouble. I watched her in amazement through my half-closed eyes. First, she took out her teeth and scrubbed them before dropping the plates into a cup of water. Next she terrified me by squeezing out her left eye and giving it a thorough swabbing. I didn't know that eyes, even glass eyes, could ever be taken from the sockets. Then she braided her long black hair, crawled into a red outing flannel nightgown, turned out the light, and ordered me to stop snooping and go to sleep.

He laughed. "Why we all recovered was a mystery to me. I think maybe it was because of the way she would sling her cuss words around; to the coal man for more fuel, to the milkman for extra milk, to the druggist for medicine, and to old man Heller for whisky. Poor Heller—he was well named. They found him slumped over the counter of the cigar store where he swept up every morning. Customers didn't pay any attention—thought he was just on another drunk. But it turned out that he was dead—from a stroke."

I glanced at the big clock on the wall. Nate would not be arriving with the mail for another twenty minutes, and Leslie, a leisurely sort of person, was still wrapped up in his story about the Boilermaker. "Doc King," he went on, "told me one of the funniest tales about her that I ever heard. After the flu began to ease, he moved his practice to Denver, opening an office in one of the new exclusive medical buildings on Tremont Street. He was a personable man and made friends quickly. Among them were some of the wealthy influential social leaders of the city. His practice kept him busy. People in the District seldom saw him unless they looked him up whenever they made a trip to Denver.

"One midwinter day," he said, "he returned from lunch to find two patients waiting in his office. One was a member of that set known as the 'Sacred Thirty-six.' She had on an elegant sealskin coat and wore sparkling diamond earrings. He knew that she had an appointment. The other, of all people, was the Boilermaker, who had just dropped in. He hadn't seen her since the flu days, but no one could ever forget the Boilermaker. The Doc confessed that he was a bit nonplussed at the sight of her in dungarees, brogans, and a pork-pie hat, and puffing a long stogie. But before he could say anything, the Boilermaker had jumped up, whacked him on the backside, and almost hugged the daylights out of him. When she finally put him down again, she gave him a sharp, searching look for a moment, and then blurted out, 'Well—you goddamned son-of-a-bitch—where you been keepin' yourself all this time? How you makin' out down here with the swells? Why don't you ever come back to the Crik to see your ol' buddies? You're a hell of a frien'!"

"Oh—for heaven's sake," I gasped. "What on earth did the Doctor do with her?"

"He hustled her into his inner sanctum as quickly and politely as possible, Doc told me, and they had a friendly to-do peppered with considerable noisy profanity on the part of the Boilermaker. After a few minutes she got up to go and he let her out through a side door into the hall and walked with her to the elevator. It wouldn't have surprised him, he declared afterward, if his other patient had passed out from shock. But she was still waiting with a quizzical smile on her face. He apologized for his delay and explained that Mrs. Heller, or the Boilermaker as she was called in Cripple Creek, was a friend whom he had drafted as a nurse during the flu. 'She's a wonderful woman,' he said, 'and saved many lives in that awful epidemic.' I guess Doc King," Leslie went on, "was pretty much worried for fear he'd lost his swank patient for good."

He sat looking out a window for a moment. "You never can tell about people, no matter how long you live and work among them. I guess that's what makes them so everlastingly interesting. Doc King told me that it must have been six or seven months after the Boilermaker incident that he happened to sit next to his socialite patient at a dinner party. He felt the sudden urge to remind her of their first meeting and to apologize for Mrs. Heller's language. The patient told him that she didn't mind it at all and went on to say that her early years had been spent up in Leadville, where her husband's money came from, and then added that because of the considerate and friendly way he had treated the Boilermaker, she had decided he was to be her family physician."

Leslie got up from his chair, stretched his arms, and laughed. "The Boilermaker was a rare person. She was a

[154]

diamond in the rough, with the tongue of a mucker and the heart of an angel. We'll never see the likes of her again—the Good Lord threw away the mold after she was cast."

# XII

# The Interrupted Summer

It was nearing the end of September 1952. Frosts had yellowed the quaking aspens on the lower slopes of Mount Pisgah. And the days were growing cooler, too cool for comfort in my lightweight California clothing. Soon, I thought wistfully, I would have to pack my suitcases and say farewell to my friends and the land of my childhood.

Bob Ragle had carried the last bound volume of the Cripple Creek *Times* from the Mill's attic. Compared with all the others I had leafed through, it seemed thin and emaciated. The year was 1919, months after the Armistice had been signed and war stories had been shoved to the back pages. But Peace Treaties did not apply to the Spanish Influenza, which was still taking a heavy toll in the western states. The District, already hard hit by war casualties, had been further decimated by what had come to be called "the black plague," because of the coffins that piled up at the alley doors of mortuaries. Camps like Elkton, Midway, and Independence, once prosperous communities, had been largely deserted. Only the towns of Cripple Creek and Victor were left to rebuild the future just as in the early days after the great fires.

I had gone faithfully every day to the Mill, first on the bus with Nate and later back and forth with Bob Ragle. I had developed a kind of affection for the dusty structure that sprawled terrace-like at the head of Arequa Gulch. The rhythmic pounding of the stamps was like the drumbeat of music, and the sweetish smell of the cyanide vats took me back to the happy years with my husband and the mill he built at the Rainbow Mine in Eastern Oregon. I was my father's daughter; mining was in the blood. I had wandered far in a different direction since leaving Cripple Creek a half century ago to enter college. But memories of those early years lingered on. The thought of saying good-by to the old-timers whom I had rediscovered filled me with sadness.

I had grown especially fond of Agnes Dewar and her rolling Scotch accent. As the day of my departure approached, she seemed to cling to me with a kind of desperation in her voice. She spoke of having no friends in camp after Millie Laveley and Lila Lovelace died; she dreaded the long winter alone with Jack. I went downstairs to chat with her the evening before I left. We pulled our chairs close to the furnace to catch the warmth and nipped a little Scotch brandy which she evidently kept hidden from her brother to use for rare occasions.

"Sometimes he acts queer," she said with a weather eye on the door. "I can't make 'im out," she went on, "and often I'm afraid of 'im. When he gets a mad up, he's mean and threatens to beat me." She choked and wiped the tears from her eyes with her apron. "He'll see," she sobbed quietly, "I'm not goin' to stand for it much longer. One of these fine days I'm takin' my savin's and goin' home to the Old Country—"

"But Agnes," I put in, "he's not young any more. You

told me once that he was almost eighty. You couldn't go off and leave him to shift for himself, with nobody in camp to take care of him if he got sick."

"The Masonic Lodge would see to that," she said shrewdly. "I guess I've done my bit of all right by 'im—"

Suddenly the front door opened and I heard steps coming down the long hall. "That's 'im now," Agnes whispered putting a finger to her lips. "He's early tonight—maybe don't feel so good—"

"Give him a draft of your delicious Scotch," I suggested. "That should set him up." But instead, she hurriedly slipped the bottle back to its hiding place, saying that liquor was bad for him because it always brought on one of his spells. I hadn't seen much of Jack since moving to the Hoot Mon. He seemed to spend most of the time at his souvenir stand, snoozing or looking up and down Bennett Avenue even when there wasn't a tourist to be found the full length of the street. Occasionally I would see him passing the time of day with one or two aged fellows on the sunny steps of Troy Wade's Hardware Store. Once or twice I tried to chat with him and asked about his collection of specimens. But he acted aloof and turned away as if he wished to be let alone.

I got up to go when I saw him coming in. What Agnes had said gave me an eerie sort of feeling. I didn't want to risk being around in case he should unexpectedly "get a mad on" when he found me visiting with his sister. But to my surprise he greeted me cordially and urged me to stay and talk about old times. "Aggie tells me you remember when I used to put on my tartans, as a young fella, and march in all the big parades, playing my bagpipe. I guess I was the only one in the District who could make music on a doodle-sack." He smiled and I saw a trace of the fetching dimple in his cheek that used to thrill the young girls of my age.

[158]

"Those were great days," he said, his gray eyes twinkling in recollection. "We'll never see 'em again—"

"You cut quite a swath," I said, grateful for his genial spirits, "swinging along in your white spats, Highland kilt, a tasseled sporran, and a quilled bonnet cocked jauntily on the back of your head. No one could ever forget you!"

Even Agnes laughed until the ready tears came again to be dried on her apron. Jack suggested that she make us coffee and serve some of the scones left over from supper. Apparently I had opened up a rich retrospective vein and he continued in a meandering sort of fashion to talk about some of his most exciting memories. "I was clerkin' in Roberts' Grocery," he said, "the time the second big fire of 1896 wiped out that end of camp. Poor old man Roberts— he was in a peck of trouble with his son Phil, who was livin' with Mexican Jennie in a shack up in Poverty Gulch. One day she shot 'im dead—claimed he'd double-crossed her on a lease—" Jack went on with a hint of relish, "She plugged him full of bullets and then escaped over the mountains to Mexico and joined up with Villa's rebels. Teller County raised hell when Sheriff von Phul used the taxpayers' money to go way down there and bring 'er back for trial! Nobody around camp had any use for Phil Roberts. They said Mexican Jennie gave 'im what he had comin' an' do you know, by God, the jury let 'er go scot free!" Jack and I had a good laugh over the pioneers' sense of quick justice. "Tell about the celebration the day the County was divided," Agnes interrupted, "and you dressed up in your kilt and bonnet and rode on a float advertising Dewar's Black and White Whisky. That was before I come to the Crik," she said aside to me. "He musta been a scream—"

Jack chuckled to himself and it was evident that he was eager to recall that memorable event. I had read a good deal about it in the old newspapers but saw no mention of Jack's name.

The day was March 23, 1899. Up to that time, the famous mining camp was located in El Paso County, a kind of Orphan Annie begging tax-crumbs of Colorado Springs, the county seat. It took a long and bitter political fight by Cripple Creekers to push a bill through the legislature, establishing a new county, named Teller, after Henry M. Teller, Colorado's popular United States Senator. The area included slices of Fremont County to the south, El Paso to the east, and in the center, all of the fabulously rich mining District. The town of Cripple Creek had been selected as the county seat and plans were under way to build the impressive, red brick County Court House where Viola Oliver and George Coplen, among others, had held forth for so many years.

"I'd like to hear the story—please go on," I said encouragingly. "It must have been a great day for you and the greatest ever for the District since the arrival of the first Florence & Cripple Creek train in 1894!"

He poured himself another cup of coffee, relit his pipe, and settled back in his chair. "It was the Masons in camp that cooked up the idea," he began. "They'd heard somewheres that I was kin to Lord Dewar, the rich distiller in Glasgow," he puffed up proudly, "and they persuaded the distributors in Denver to donate several cases of little sample bottles of their famous brew to be passed out from a float to the crowds watching the parade along Bennett Avenue on County Division Day.

"So the Lodge fixed up a truck decorated with bunting and Scotch and American flags and put me on a small platform with open cases of whisky piled all around. In between tunes on the bagpipe, I'd sling handfuls of those samples in all directions. How the folks scrambled for 'em in the street!" Agnes shook with delight as he described it. "I never knew the Crik had so many people," he went on, "'til I saw 'em chasin' after that whisky wagon—hundreds of kids, old men on crutches, and girls from the row, yellin' and screamin' their heads off, tryin' to catch the bottles, fightin' for 'em when they landed on the ground, swingin' up on the float 'til it almost tipped over! Pretty soon, I tried a few samples, myself; thought I might as well join in the fun. It was mighty good stuff—best I'd ever tasted. Then I began to slip extra snorters under my belt and all hell broke loose." He rocked back and forth in his chair weak from laughter. "So help me, I never knew when that goddamn parade was over. The Masons scooped me up, they said, and carried me off to the Lodge and put me to bed!"

"I never got through wishin' that I'd been in camp and could have had a few nips of that fine brew, myself!" Agnes added rather longingly. I was beginning to suspect that perhaps "nipping" was another of her problems.

I glanced at the alarm clock on the shelf above the sink; it was almost midnight. I expected to take the bus, next morning, for Colorado Springs in time to connect with the plane for Los Angeles and still had a few last things to pack. As I started to go, Jack began to rummage through a drawer in the table. "Hold on a minute," he said, "here's something to remember me by!" And he handed me a postcard picture of himself looking pleased and elated in his full Scotch regalia, with the bagpipe slung vainly over his shoulder. He watched me as I took it admiringly and thanked him. "It's just as I recall you in all the Fourth of July and Labor Day parades. You haven't changed a great deal."

A strange distant expression came into his eyes. "Aw—go—on—you're jokin'," he said. "You can't fool me. I'm pushin' eighty—gotta face it—ask Aggie here—" he said, nodding toward her. "She's not the same either—never used to talk all the time about goin' back to the Old Country the way she does now—but I'll see her in hell first." He managed a laugh and said something about having to get down to the souvenir stand early to straighten up things before the customers started lining up. We shook hands and I halfway promised to return to Cripple Creek the coming summer, provided they had a vacancy at the Hoot Mon and he would tell me more of his stories.

Agnes turned on the hall light and walked with me to the foot of the stairs. "He's been real sociable tonight," she said in a low voice. "I can't remember when I've seen him so jolly. Let me know in time if you ever want the apartment again. I'll see to it that there's room for you."

Nate opened the bus window before we left the hotel and I waved to her all the way down Third Street until he turned out of sight up Bennett Avenue to Old Town. I couldn't get her from my mind for a long time. It seemed to me that she was the tragic embodiment of the loneliness and desolation I felt had gradually crept over Cripple Creek.

I planned to spend the winter in North Hollywood going through my voluminous notes taken from reading the back numbers of the newspapers and in talking with many old-timers. They had to be sorted out, put in order, and somehow woven into a story. I had not yet decided on the form it would take or the point of view. But as the months and years passed, with many trials and errors in writing and numerous revisions, I began to feel the need of returning to the District for another few weeks to cover the ground I had neglected and to visit with other interesting old-timers whom I had overlooked. But again I was blocked by finances and could see no way of taking another trip to Colorado.

Then, one day, a letter came from a classmate of mine at Colorado College, reminding me that it was 1956 and telling of arrangements that were being made to observe the

Golden Jubilee of our class at the coming June Commencement. On the spur of the moment, I enclosed it in one of my letters to Lowell, saying lightly that it hardly seemed possible that fifty years had passed since my graduation. True to his character, he wrote at once urging me to go to the reunion. "And while you are so close," he added enthusiastically, "why not make it to Cripple Creek for a few weeks and look up some fascinating people you missed. I can think of any number of them—Vern Peiffer; Bill Kyner, my former newspaper boss; Tom Rolofson; Harry Gehm, Carlton's long-time, confidential secretary; and you should have a long session with Ethel Carlton, Bert's beautiful widow, to name only a few. Some of them may have moved to the Springs or Denver, but they are still within easy reach. You could get more than enough material," he wrote persuasively, "to fill a half-dozen books."

It was about the middle of April and with Lowell's tangible urging I decided to make reservations for the Golden Jubilee and also to inquire of Agnes about a vacancy at the Hoot Mon. If my former apartment were going to be available, I said, I would arrive on the tenth of June and possibly stay two months. Word came within a week assuring me of the apartment and adding that the rent had been raised to fifty dollars a month, with bedding, "payable in advance." I sent the check immediately and told her a Denver friend would be driving me up from the Springs and that we should arrive early in the afternoon.

I had a fine feeling about the way things had worked out. Commencement festivities had been heart-warming, and after the good-bys were over, my friend and I set out in her shiny yellow Buick through the Garden of the Gods to Manitou and up Ute Pass. By driving leisurely and enjoying the familiar sights we expected to reach Cripple Creek at around two o'clock, soon enough for her to start back to

Denver in good time and to give me a chance to unpack, chat with Agnes, and do some marketing for dinner. It was one of those scintillating days so common to Colorado in summer. Rugged peaks notched the azure sky, meadow larks sang from the telephone poles, and the scent of wild lupine and sweet alyssum filled the air.

But the most stirring of all was the thought that I was going back to Cripple Creek and the cozy apartment at the Hoot Mon. I could almost see Agnes standing in the doorway, in a fresh gingham dress and white apron, waiting to welcome me. But the door was closed; apparently I had arrived earlier than she expected. My friend helped me in with the two suitcases and started back at once on the long trip to Denver. I went down the hall and knocked at the Dewar apartment. No one seemed to be home so I hurried upstairs thinking that Agnes was busy getting my rooms in readiness, but when I opened the door, I was met by a swarm of enormous green flies buzzing and bouncing against the skylight, and a sickening odor unlike anything I had ever smelled before, choked and smothered me. The place was in a shambles. It looked as if it hadn't been cleaned for weeks. How unlike Agnes! She must have misunderstood my letter.

I decided to go down Bennett Avenue to look for Jack at his souvenir stand. Halfway up the block a doddering man came limping toward me, one of the old codgers, I guessed, who would surely be able to tell me where Agnes had gone. But as he drew nearer, I realized with a shock that it was Jack Dewar. I scarcely recognized him. His spotted, soiled clothes hung like rags on his stooped body; his face was thin and unshaven. He squinted at me with rheumy eyes; it was plain that he didn't know me.

"What's the matter, Jack," I asked, stopping. "Are you sick?"

"Got rheumatiz," he said feebly, rubbing his knee. "Who are you?"

I told him my name and said that I had lived at the Hoot Mon a few summers before. "You remember—I had the upstairs apartment. I wrote Agnes that I wanted it again for a couple of months. She is expecting me. Where can I find her?"

He seemed confused; he had also grown very deaf. "Agnes—Who did you say you was?"

I told him again in a louder voice and asked where Agnes had gone.

"Why—she went to California—been there 'bout three weeks—"

"That's where I live, Jack," I said, trying to set him straight. "Is Agnes in camp or has she gone to visit her friend in Florence?"

"No," he said angrily, "it's none of your business. She'll be back in a couple of days an' take care of you."

I mentioned her promise to furnish the bedding. "Did she say anything to you about it before she went away?"

He shook his head impatiently and started to amble off. Then he turned and said: "There's some blankets on the cot where she sleeps. Come in an' help yourself—"

Something told me that it wouldn't be a good idea. "Never mind," I said, "I'll rent them again from the Imperial until Agnes returns home."

I felt vaguely troubled and walked on down to the post office to ask the clerk if Agnes had given any forwarding address when she left camp. He looked surprised and said he was not aware that she had gone away. Then he added that Jack always picked up any mail that came for her.

"Have you seen him lately?" I persisted.

The clerk couldn't remember. The tourist season was getting under way, crowding things a bit.

"Somebody had better keep an eye on him," I said earnestly. "I met him up the street a little while ago and couldn't believe my eyes. He looked lost and as if he might drop dead of starvation almost any minute."

The clerk appeared concerned; he said he would take it up with the Lodge at the meeting next week. I went on to the market to lay in a few supplies, mostly disinfectants, deodorants, and fly poison. The door to the back apartment was ajar when I returned and I could see Jack stirring the furnace with a long poker. He called out something to me about picking up some blankets, but I pretended not to hear and went on upstairs.

I had opened all the windows before going downtown but Cripple Creek's vaunted fresh air was not potent enough to overcome the nauseating, pervasive stench of whatever Jack had been trying to burn in the furnace. I sprayed deodorants all over the place, but they had no effect. I flushed the toilet with detergents and disinfectants but to no avail. I assaulted the horrible green insects with fly-killers, only to see new squadrons dashing their wings against the ceiling window. Finally I realized that it was out of the question even to open a can of soup for a meal and I went over to the hotel for dinner.

Sleep was impossible that night and at five o'clock in the morning when the pink glow of the sun heartened me a little, I got up and made a pot of strong coffee, and resolved to spend another day looking for Agnes. First of all, I would ask Nate when he stopped his bus at the Imperial, around nine o'clock, if he remembered Agnes Dewar going out of camp with him in the last few weeks.

"No," he said, scratching the back of his head. "If she'd been on the bus I'd a-noticed her 'specially—she never went no place that I know of."

"Maybe she drove to Florence, or Divide, or some other town with a friend."

"Taint likely," he said casually. "She never had many friends, as I know of—" He looked at his wrist watch and released the brake. "I'll let you know if I hear anything."

Jack met me in the hall when I came back to the Hoot Mon. "You want to come in now an' get them blankets?" he asked. "Plenty of 'em there on the cot—you can pick out what you need."

I explained that I had decided to rent bedding from the hotel until Agnes came home and I was quite comfortable. It seemed wise not to annoy or risk angering him in any way. He rubbed his watery eyes with his hand as if trying to recollect. "I'm lookin' for her sure on Friday—"

It was a waste of breath to try to settle anything with him, even to question the reason for the fetid odor and hordes of flies. I determined to continue my quest for news of Agnes and went to the one remaining bank in the District to ask if she had deposited my check or withdrawn any money from her account. I had known the cashier from my first visit to camp and he spoke freely. The bank had no record of Agnes Dewar ever having deposited or withdrawn money. He laughed and said, "She probably keeps it in her woollies." But I couldn't see the joke. I spoke of the flies and the odor and told him frankly that I suspected she had met with foul play and that her body was hidden somewhere in the Hoot Mon, probably in the furnace.

He smiled with kindly tolerance. "That odor is awful at times," he said. "All of us in camp have been bothered with it now and then. It comes from defective sewers. As for the flies—few people up here have screens—the season is so short—and they soon vanish if you keep after them with poison spray. Just be careful not to get any on your bacon and eggs!" He put his hand on my shoulder as I turned to

[167]

go. "Don't be anxious about Jack," he said paternally. "He's old and feeble but quite harmless. Agnes will be back all right—if he says so."

I returned to my apartment a bit easier in mind. Nick, the policeman, a powerfully built fellow, was just coming out the front door. We talked for a moment on the sidewalk. Leslie Wilkinson, the postmaster, had told him to look in on Jack and to let the Lodge know if he needed anything. "He's okay," Nick said, "just a little off in the upper story due to his age. When Agnes gets home and makes some scones for him, he'll be all right. I'm taking him to supper tonight down at the Gold Coin lunchroom—"

"But what about this strange and sickening stench?" I put in. "It's unlike anything I've ever known—"

"It's those sewers again," he said. "I'll take the matter up with the mayor in the morning. I don't know what the hell we're going to do about 'em. The camp ain't got money for repairs—" He gave a hopeless shrug and started away.

"I must talk with you—so Jack won't hear," I said, gripped with sudden fear. "Come upstairs with me for a minute." He smiled indulgently and followed me to the small parlor. I had noticed when I first arrived two days before that the door to the attic was wide open. I had closed it quietly and avoided going into the room again. Nick listened patiently while I told him of my suspicions. He wanted to know if I had ever heard them fighting when I had lived there before. I said no and explained that their apartment was pretty well isolated from the rest of the house. "You've let yourself get all upset," he said soothingly. "Jack wouldn't hurt a flea. Nothing's wrong with 'im that a square meal wouldn't cure."

"Would you examine their bedrooms?" I asked, "just to make sure about Agnes?"

"No. I ain't got a search warrant—"

"Then before you leave," I urged, "would you mind going up to the attic and taking a look around?"

"Sure—if it'll make you feel any better." He seemed rather put out with me but even so took his big flashlight and climbed the stairs. I could hear him shoving boxes around, kicking loose boards, slamming lids shut. "It's like I told you," he said, coming down again. "Everything's dusty but okay. Forget it or somebody'll have to send for Doc Denman to give you the once-over."

Nick's reassurance calmed me considerably, enough to enable me to sleep for a few hours, before being wakened with the dawn by that penetrating smell and the beetle-like flies zooming against the skylight. It was Friday, the beginning of my third day at the Hoot Mon and still there were no signs of Agnes' return. If she didn't show up on the afternoon bus, I thought, it might be a good idea to go up to Dr. Denman's office in the hospital on Church Hill. Perhaps I am unduly nervous, I said to myself, and my imagination has got the better of me. Surely all these old-timers can't be mistaken. They were probably gossiping and making fun of my notions and doubts about Jack and Agnes.

With this cheerful thought, I decided to go to the market for a few items I'd forgotten the first time. The clerk, a middle-aged woman who knew everybody in camp and most of what was going on, asked me at once if anything had been heard of Agnes Dewar—when she was expected back from California. "I hope it's mighty soon," she said. "Jack looks like he is on his last legs. He's got crazy as a loon lately; two or three weeks ago he came in and bought a padlock. Nobody could figure out what he wanted it for. Funny— Agnes going away like that—never telling a soul—"

There was something in the way the woman talked that sent shivers through me. I was trembling like a leaf. I asked her to have the groceries sent and I made my way directly to Dr. Denman's office. At least, he could give me something to quiet my nerves. He was an agreeable, sympathetic person who had practiced many years in Teller County. Now he was the only physician left. He listened patiently as I started from the beginning to tell him of my suspicions since arriving at the Hoot Mon and finding no signs of Agnes anywhere; it was as if she had vanished forever. He listened without interrupting and at last said, smiling in the kindly manner to which I had become used, "You're in a highly disturbed state of mind, my dear Mrs. Lee, due, no doubt, to overwork or worry, and moles have come to look like mustangs."

I was on the verge of weeping and struggled to control my emotions. I realized that a single tear would confirm the doctor's diagnosis; he might even want to send me to the hospital! "But how do you account for that frightful odor?" I persisted. "And all those big green flies—they seem to get worse by the hour!"

"Sewers," he claimed. "Nothing but broken sewers. They give us a lot of trouble in camp—"

"But what about Jack's strange behavior?"

"He's senescent and muddled—he's lived too long—but he's a mild sort of fellow and wouldn't harm a soul, least of all Agnes. When she gets back and feeds him properly, he'll be all right. Meanwhile, maybe a prescription for phenobarbital will enable you to relax and get a good night's sleep." He went into another room and fixed a bottle of pink solution. "Take a teaspoonful when you go to bed and if it doesn't work in an hour, take another. That should fix you up!"

Agnes did not come in on the bus as Jack had predicted. He said he had got mixed up and it was the following day that he expected her. I went to the Imperial again for dinner and returned fairly early to my apartment. Jack was poking around, as usual, in the furnace. He called out something, through the half-open door, about getting some blankets, but I hurried upstairs without answering and turned the key in the door. Then it occurred to me that Jack would undoubtedly have a pass key and all my old terror returned. I ran to my bedroom window thinking that I might jump out, but that would have meant death or crippling for life.

I pushed all the movable furniture against the hall door, took two teaspoonfuls of phenobarbital, put the bottle on the dresser, and crawled under the quilts. I repeated a double dosage every hour until well after midnight, but if anything, it only made me more alert and watchful. The wind had come up and was blowing hard, whipping the lace curtains in and out of the window, banging loose doors and chimney pipes. The full, pale moon hung in a clear sky, casting weird shadows through the skylight. Suddenly I sat up stiff with fear, thinking that there was someone in the hall turning the knob. I groped for the cord to pull on the light, determined to face it out with Jack at the risk of being killed. "What do you want?" I called firmly. "Go away, go away, I tell you, or I'll shoot you." But there was no response—only the wind rattling the door and somewhere in the distance the piercing wail of a donkey.

It was almost four o'clock by my watch and I went to the kitchen to make a pot of coffee. Reason seemed to return under its comforting warmth. One thing was certain: I couldn't endure another night at the Hoot Mon.

I gave Jack the groceries and a new supply of deodorants and moved over to the hotel the next morning. He acted quite relieved and reconciled when I explained that it was to stay only until Agnes came home. He even offered to help the bellboy carry my two suitcases across the street.

It was like heaven that night, being among friends at the Imperial. I enjoyed one of François' tasty dinners and later even took in the show in The Gold Bar Room Theatre—a melodrama called *After Dark, Neither Wife, Maid Nor Widow*. For a few blissful hours I had forgotten about Agnes and her whereabouts, and when I went to bed it was to spend the whole night in blessed, drugless sleep.

Around ten o'clock the next morning, as I started to take a leisurely walk down Bennett Avenue to the post office, I saw Nick standing outside by the open door at the Hoot Mon. From the look on his face, I knew instantly that something was wrong and I hurried across to speak to him. He was pale and his hand trembled when he lit a cigarette. Oddly enough, I didn't think of Agnes. "What's the trouble, Nick?" I asked. "Is Jack dead?"

He shook his head gravely. "You were right. Agnes is in there. By God, I've never seen anything like it—maggots all over the place. I've got a stomach of iron, but that stench was more than I could swallow. The Doc, the undertaker, an' the mayor are shovelin' 'er up now. Doc Denman says she's so far gone there's not much use to try to hold a post-mortem. Besides, the city hasn't got enough money for a murder trial. McMillin's'll likely hurry her out to Pisgah Graveyard. By the back road, let's hope."

"How did you happen to come here again so soon?"

"It got around camp that you'd moved out 'cause you suspicioned that Agnes' body was hid somewheres on the premises. The mayor got a search warrant an' we came up early this mornin' an' told Jack we wanted to see if the sewer was okay. We headed for the bathroom to look at the plumbin'. He followed us without sayin' a word. Then I noticed that one of the doors was padlocked. A stink was comin' through the cracks and the mayor asked 'im for the key—"

I was spellbound. "What did he do then?"

"He wouldn't give it to us. Let out a string of oaths an' told us to mind our goddamn business. We kicked in the door just the same—" Nick gagged and wiped his mouth. "So help me, there she was on a cot, her gray hair barely showin' from under a pile of blankets. We got hold of Doc Denman right away. He said she musta been dead four or five weeks. Then we sent for the undertaker." He was silent for a moment and looked off in the distance as if trying to figure out a puzzle. "Funny thing," he muttered half to himself, "we found a big straw valise under the cot full of clothes like she had packed up to go away and in the very bottom was an almost empty bottle of that Dewar Black and White Scotch Whisky—" He managed a sympathetic smile. "Guess Agnes liked to tipple every once in a while—"

Jack spent the night in jail and papers were made out the next day for him to enter the State Hospital in Pueblo. Nick drove him down and said he talked all the time, wondering why Agnes hadn't come home when she said she would. I decided to forgo spending a month or two in Cripple Creek and left the following morning for California. As I went out to climb on the bus, Nick was waiting for me in front of the hotel. "We found this among Jack's things," he said, handing me an unopened letter directed to Agnes Dewar. My name and return address were written across the back. The postmark was May 15, 1956. I tore it open and found my note reserving the apartment and enclosing my check intact for the June rent.

It struck me as I looked back from Tenderfoot Hill that a shroud of immortality lay over the fabulous old camp in which I had grown up from childhood to a young woman going away to school. Its heydays could never be fully recaptured and brought alive again, but the memories of those fantastic years would survive in the countless tales and legends told and retold, written and still to be written, the "little stories that are the small change of history."

# XIII

# New Bonanzas for Old

"The World's Greatest Gold Camp" was celebrating its Diamond Jubilee during the summer of 1966. Seventy-five years had passed since a "crazy" ranch-hand prospector named Robert "Bob" M. Womack first discovered gold in a rocky cleft of the mountains known as Poverty Gulch. Men down in Colorado City saloons were skeptical when Bob showed them his specimens streaked with silver-colored tellurides. Gold was yellow, they said, and Bob was drunk.

But curiosity got the better of some of them, mostly druggists, butchers, grocers, and one or two real estate agents. They made secret forays into the wild country the other side of Pike's Peak. None of them knew much about geology, but they took random samples of the quartz scattered here and there on Bull, Globe, and Tenderfoot hills. One maverick carpenter and sometime prospector from Colorado Springs, named W. S. Stratton, staked out a claim in Poverty Gulch and then tramped southward as far as Battle Mountain, where he put his mark on two or three other promising pieces of land, one of which later assayed $360 a ton. Since the find had been made on July 4, 1891, he called it the "Independence." But Stratton was an astute, closemouthed fellow. He told Bob Womack that he didn't think much of the District.

In spite of his secretiveness, word leaked out that "Stratton had struck pay dirt," and soon an assortment of pseudo prospectors, armed with picks and canvas sample sacks, began to scuff over the hills and stake out claims. It was like an exciting game to them and occasionally miracles of discovery happened. According to legend, two druggists from the Springs sat down near the top of Bull Hill to rest their aching feet. One of them suggested that it was all a big gamble anyhow and he tossed his hat in the air and bet he'd strike gold where it landed. He did; and the mine he called the "Pharmacist" developed into one of the richest in the District.

For some reason, the early excitement seemed to fade. Cripple Creek was slow in kindling the interest of moneyed men. Possibly it was too close to civilization to be taken seriously. The richest lodes, it was said, were usually found in remote, rugged country, inaccessible to Sunday hikers and amateurs collecting specimens. It wasn't until 1892 when the Buena Vista jackpot was discovered near Midway, up on Bull Hill, that the gold rush started with a bang. Nothing like it had ever before been seen in the West.

Bonanzas sprang up like mushrooms after a summer shower and dozens of small camps squeezed in around them, dotting the mountain slopes, cluttering the gulches. Cripple Creek, lying in a volcanic basin to the north of the District, was the most populous but Victor, six miles south and the second largest, snuggled against the sunny breast of Battle Mountain with its fabulous mines, the Portland, Strong,

Ajax, Golden Cycle, Vindicator, Findley, and Independence, forming a golden background.

Frantic men and women clamored over the mountains, hoping to repeat Stratton's find. They bothered him with questions and tried to locate claims near his properties. But he wouldn't talk much; too many people crowding around rubbed him the wrong way. He decided to sell out and go back to his trade of carpentry. He offered the Independence diggings for five hundred dollars to a twenty-five-year-old tuberculous patient in Colorado Springs, named Albert "Bert" E. Carlton. But he turned it down saying that his days were numbered and that he would have no use for a gold mine. But fate would deal different hands to these two individualists. Stratton took a second look at Battle Mountain and Poverty Gulch and decided to hang on to his properties a while longer. Shortly before the turn of the century he sold the Independence to the Venture Corporation of London for $10,000,000. Three years later he died of alcoholism. Bert Carlton extricated himself from the grave and lived on to make millions in the District's freight traffic and banking; and at his death in 1931 he controlled most of the camp's great mines which had a grand total production record of $227,000,000.

The railroads came in 1894 and 1895, first the narrow-gauge Florence & Cripple Creek from the south, and then the broad-gauge Midland Terminal from the east and north. Much later, in 1901, a third railroad, the Short Line, would lay its tracks up the steep canyons behind Cheyenne Mountain, cutting the distance and time between Colorado Springs and the District, and offering breath-taking views to tempt the tourists. Meanwhile, two electric cars, the High Line and the Low Line, wound in and out among the District mines, taking men to and from work, and their wives shopping at the big stores in Cripple Creek and Victor.

The Midland Terminal had built an imposing, red brick depot across the upper end of Bennett Avenue where it jutted into Womack Hill. Thousands of people from many parts of the world caught their first glimpse of the storied mining camp from the depot's sloping steps. It was here one night, after the show, that Primrose and Dockstader's Minstrels serenaded the returning honeymooners, Bert and Ethel Carlton, who afterward took the whole band to the National Hotel and served them magnums of champagne. From time to time the luxurious private cars of Evalyn Walsh, whose father struck it rich at the Camp Bird, over in the San Juans; or Alfred Vanderbilt; or the Gaekwar of Baroda could be seen parked on a siding of the Midland tracks above Poverty Gulch. There seemed to be no end to the lure of Cripple Creek's fantastic gold mines for the profligate, rich, and famous; and there was no limit to the sights they wanted to see, especially those down on Myers Avenue—the camp's notorious tenderloin.

Slumming parties strolled past the miserable cribs with red lamps showing in the windows, and stared at the scantily dressed prostitutes within hoping to attract business. Here and there were the shuttered parlor houses called by exotic names—the Parisian, Laura Belle's, the Mikado, and the Bon Ton. The Old Homestead, best known and highest priced, stood aloof from the others. The shades were carefully drawn to keep out the sun and a maid in white cap and apron answered the doorbell. Its elaborate balls and banquets were the talk of the camp, its girls the most beautiful, and the elite patrons the richest. Only a few yards lay between the Old Homestead and the Negro and French brothels of Poverty Gulch, but not many in search of thrills cared to risk the shooting scrapes up there and the robberies that often overtook the well-heeled sightseer.

Weekend visitors flocked to camp for Labor Day, Fourth

of July, or Decoration Day celebrations. Nowhere else, they said, could people have more fun. Flags, bunting, and wild flowers decked Bennett Avenue. Hundreds of Lodge members in full uniform marched in the big parades. The air was filled with music of the Elks' Band, the Victor Miners' Band, Cook's Drum Corps, and the Anaconda Drum Corps. Other sounds, the true sounds of Cripple Creek, added to the thump, thump of the bass drums. Mine whistles blowing, the bells of the Midland's freight engines clanging, the streetcars whining around the curve at Bennett and Second, stray dogs fighting, donkeys braying, sometimes a crash of thunder followed by deadly lightning killing men coming down the trail from the Anchoria-Leland. And often, in the dead of the night, six shots ringing out the fire alarm.

But fire, the ever-present terror of Cripple Creekers, was not particular about time or season. The most disastrous in the history of the camp occurred in April 1896. It struck twice, three days apart, and consumed most of the business and residential sections. The first one was checked at Fourth Street, barely missing the framework of the new five-story, red pressed-brick National Hotel and the Midland Depot, less than a block east. The second outbreak spread west almost to Pisgah Graveyard. But the people were not disheartened. Rebuilding started as soon as the ashes cooled. Every structure on Bennett Avenue was of brick and each had a different trim. The National Hotel was completed and became the center of the District's social and extramarital activities, which sometimes ended in scandal and even murder, justified under the "unwritten law."

The Imperial Hotel up on Third Street, across from the Post Office and Telephone buildings, competed for the National's overflow and permanent roomers. Its clientele consisted largely of young engineers, lawyers, and doctors who hadn't yet made their stakes. It came into its own, however, as the leading hostelry when, due to financial wreckage, the National was torn down in 1919 to save taxes. The Imperial had weathered the stormy years of the long killing strike of 1903–4 and the subsequent closing of some of the big mines. There were signs of the camp's dying when the Western Federation of Miners lost and was driven from the District, and its members forced to look elsewhere for jobs. Then, there was a sudden shot of adrenalin in the arm of the mining industry. It happened in November 1914. A pioneer Dutchman, named Richard Roelofs, struck a vug of gold at the Cresson Mine over on Raven Hill that sparked fresh hope in the hearts of other old-timers. Before Christmas Day the crystalline walls of the vug had produced $700,000 and soon Richard Roelofs' name had been added to Cripple Creek's list of some forty or fifty millionaires, and the Cresson had become a famous member of Bert Carlton's family of bonanzas.

But it took more than one great producer to restore the camp to prosperity. Clouds of World War I had darkened Europe and finally in 1917 engulfed the United States. Cripple Creek's young men changed their mine overalls to army uniforms and marched away to battle. At last, when the shooting was about over, the Spanish Influenza sweeping the country hit Cripple Creek with deadly force and plunged it into the shadow of a ghost town. The only railroad left was the Midland Terminal; few travelers any more included a visit to "The World's Greatest Gold Camp" in their itinerary.

The Cripple Creek District, exhausted by the inroads of war, influenza, and dwindling production, lay dormant for more than two decades. Many of the once great mines had closed down or were being worked by leasers. Water flooded the deeper shafts and Carlton conceived the idea of building two costly drainage tunnels. But the price of gold had cheapened, resulting in a further cut in profits. Only two or three of the former giants were able to keep up production. Again Carlton tried to revive the camp by planning a two-million-dollar cyanide mill over in Arequa Gulch, to treat the vast dumps that sprawled down the mountainsides. He now owned or controlled every industry left in the District, except the Strong Mine, just above Victor. But this abiding ambition turned out to be a mockery. He died, together with most of his mines, and Ethel, his widow, carried out his dream by erecting the mill in his memory. For a few years, men who had been long out of work had jobs again and the camp enjoyed a slight measure of prosperity. But finally the dumps, too, yielded up their last traces of gold and the Carlton Mill was padlocked in 1962.

Some time before, a new breed of tenderfoot began to try his luck in the ghostly old camp. The forerunners were Blevins Davis and a small group of associates from Colorado Springs where he lived. Davis had once been one of Lowell Thomas' page boys at the National Broadcasting Company in New York City. Later he married a widow who lived in a mansion in Broadmoor. She died soon afterward and left him her huge fortune. He was at a loss to find constructive ways to spend all his wealth. Someone suggested that he develop Cripple Creek into a famous cultural center and summer resort, on the order of Central City. Instead of opera, however, Davis proposed to feature a "Theatre of the Ballet." But the altitude of some ten thousand feet made that seem impractical. Instead, a weekly newspaper, called the *Cripple Creek Gold Rush* was revived to stir public interest in the District. All of the railroads had been wrecked and their roadbeds turned into highways. Davis bought the Midland Terminal Depot with the idea of making it a museum. A crusade was started among the townspeople to repair and repaint some of the tottery houses and offer them for rent to summer residents. Excitement quickened the steps of people. Once again hope beckoned from the horizon above Tenderfoot Hill. But as the months passed, Blevins Davis seemed to lose interest in Cripple Creek. Other more prestigious missions called him to Europe and South America. And the Midland Terminal windows remained boarded up.

Around 1946, two enterprising young people, Wayne and Dorothy Mackin, arrived to look over the situation. They speculated that the dying camp had possibilities as an attraction for tourists. There were no hotels left except the Imperial, which was on its last legs, and Wayne and Dorothy managed to scrape up enough savings to buy it. They began the refurbishings, a room at a time in the style of the Nineties, with the addition of modern plumbing and comfortable beds; and Dorothy made a point of serving her home-cooked meals. They faced a Herculean job with limited resources. Profits never seemed to catch up with debts. Prospects improved, however, after they engaged a French chef, named François, to preside over the kitchen. Night after night he lured the elite of Denver and Colorado Springs to camp with his rare gourmet dinners. But something more was needed to make a go of the Imperial.

Dorothy had always been rather stage-struck and one night she said to her husband, "Why don't we turn the basement of the Hotel into a 'Little Theatre' specializing in melodrama?" Wayne seemed to think it a great idea until he got a good look at the musty basement. In its day, it had served as wine cellar, storeroom, mortuary, and makeshift jail during the last strike. There wasn't much to start with, but the Mackins pitched in and renovated the place from cement floor to rafters. They installed a bar and scattered small tables around where audiences could sit and drink steins of beer as they booed villains or applauded beautiful, sad-eyed heroines. The cozy little playhouse was dubbed "The Gold Bar Room Theatre."

The first show opened in June 1948, with a heart-rending performance of *Curfew Villain,* put on by the Piper Players. Popular pianist Max Morath of Colorado Springs, in shirt sleeves, fancy armlets, and straw sailor perched on the back of his head, hammered out "She's Only a Bird in a Gilded Cage" and other tinpan alley tunes of the early 1900s. Dorothy took charge of the wardrobe and Wayne acted as bartender. Crowds from the towns and cities on the plains below flocked to the old camp in Fords, Lincolns, and Cadillacs to enjoy one of François' exotic creations and later take in the melodrams. When receipts were counted at the end of the season, it was found that eleven thousand people had dined at the Imperial and cheered and laughed and brushed away errant tears as they watched *Curfew Villain* in The Gold Bar Room Theatre.

Skeptics in camp began to change their minds and saw opportunities for themselves in the Mackin success. The owners of the Molly Kathleen Mine, not far from the highway down Tenderfoot Hill, make a bid for tourists by taking them one thousand feet underground, at $1.00 admission, to let them sniff the damp earth, lead them through drifts, and pass around small souvenir specimens of ore taken from the stopes. Hundreds of tenderfeet took advantage of the new experience. It turned out to be a veritable jackpot for the Molly Kathleen, and the El Paso Mine on Beacon Hill soon followed suit.

One of the most ambitious of all the ventures was the grading of a two-lane, gravel road winding more than two miles to the summit of Mount Pisgah. No one thought it could be done except Postmaster Leslie Wilkinson, his wife Ruby, and a few stouthearted local men, who were the prime movers. This eleven-thousand-foot, cone-shaped peak rose like a giant monument just behind Pisgah Graveyard. And when the highway opened in 1956, long lines of visitors in cars wound snake-like up the slope to catch the breathtaking view from the top. Off to the south were the glistening Sangre de Cristo reaching into distant New Mexico, toward the west could be seen the Collegiate ranges of the Continental Divide, standing out clear and majestic; and to the east, only a stone's throw away, it seemed, Pike's Peak, towering 14,110 feet, kept watch over the rampart-hills of the Cripple Creek District.

The *Cripple Creek Gold Rush,* that interesting little weekly which Blevins Davis once brought back to life and published, had widened its circulation under its editor, Richard Johnson, and later, Roy G. Robinson. Newcomers were attracted to the camp. They bought up some of the aged houses and turned them into charming homes. The shrinking population had sharply increased from eight hundred to a thousand during the summer season. The Midland Terminal Depot, at last, became a reality as a museum, displaying many memorabilia of the early days, from mining tools to women's dresses, with a replica on the third floor of a Victorian living room, such as might have been found in 1900 on exclusive Eaton Avenue. Victor, not to be outdone by its long-time rival, opened a museum in the boyhood home of Lowell Thomas, showing mementoes of his early youth in that town.

But the most seductive of all of the District's new museums was the once infamous parlor house known far and wide as the Old Homestead. The faded pink brick building, where I had stayed with the Bob Ragles for a few weeks in 1952, had been bought by the Fred Mentzers and restored to a semblance of its original appearance. The furnishings were carried out painstakingly, with chairs and sofas upholstered in red; and soft velvet draperies hung at the windows.

The wallpaper in the banquet hall, which was ordered from Europe by Pearl De Vere, one of its most beautiful madams, was still a fresh, woodsy green. A grand piano, together with an Edison phonograph and a morning-glory speaker, could be seen in the back parlor. Manikins, dressed as daughters of joy in elegant gowns typical of the period, were arranged here and there, giving a feeling of life to the vacant rooms. Their names are forgotten but those of the gorgeous madams—Hazel Vernon, Lola Livingston, Georgia Hayden, Dolly Stars, and Pearl De Vere—are immortalized in the history of Cripple Creek's flamboyant gold-rush years.

The Diamond Jubilee in 1966 drew hundreds of tourists to see and participate in the summer's events. Wayne and Dorothy Mackin were opening their 19th season with a thrilling melodrama, called *Fear in the Forest* by Steele MacKaye. Tickets were sold out weeks in advance and last season's attendance of thirty thousand promised to be duplicated. In view of this new gold rush, the Imperial expanded its housing facilities. A motel was built; the old county hospital over on the Placer west of town was acquired and remodeled into an attraction called Travel Park Hospitality House. The Hoot Mon Apartments, where I had spent three days and nights of terror with the ghost of Agnes Dewar in 1956, had been bought and renovated as quarters for actors and members of the staff of The Gold Bar Room Theatre.

That summer marked the seventy-fifth anniversary since the discovery of the first bonanza. Not many old-timers would be seen among the crowds watching the Donkey Derby Day parade on Bennett Avenue, or the finish of the "World's Championship Donkey Race" over a six-mile route from Victor to Cripple Creek, or the annual Mount Pisgah Motorcycle Road Race, or eating their fill at the Community Barbecue in the little City Park across from the County Court House. Their faces have passed from the familiar scene. Jack Dewar, who had lived from parade to parade most of his life, died after two months in the State Hospital down in Pueblo, still awaiting Agnes' return from California "any day now," to take him home to the Hoot Mon in Cripple Creek. I shall never see the Olivers again, or spend jolly evenings laughing over bygone days with Grace Eads (she had died sometime before the McMillin Building in Victor at last burned down). I shall never visit again with George Coplen or with handsome Vern Peiffer or Ethel Carlton or stricken Tom Sharkey. I shall never feel a catch in my throat when I see Bill Kyner, the bravest of them all, who after losing both hands and feet from frostbite operated his Isabella lease on Bull Hill from a wheelchair and made a modest fortune. Dr. W. W. King was in his nineties when he put away his stethoscope for the last time. And nevermore would I chuckle with Ben Hill telling me the story of Carry Nation and the night she gave Johnny Nolon's saloon a "smashing" that made headlines in all the country's newspapers.

These and many others with whom I talked about the gold-rush years had "crossed the range" as miners used to say, leaving behind only warm memories of their wit and kindness, their folly and wisdom, and a rich heritage of unforgettable and sometimes unbelievable tales from their recollections.

# INDEX

J4

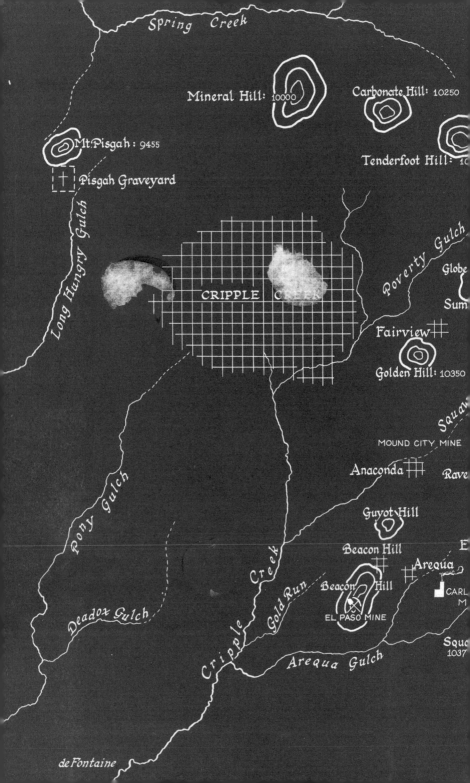